Critical Interventions: A Forum for Social Analysis
General Editor: Bruce Kapferer

MIGRATION, DEVELOPMENT, AND TRANSNATIONALIZATION
A Critical Stance

Edited by

Nina Glick Schiller

and

Thomas Faist

Berghahn Books
NEW YORK • OXFORD
www.berghahnbooks.com

Published in 2010 by
Berghahn Books

www.berghahnbooks.com

© 2010 Berghahn Books
Reprinted in 2011, 2012

Library of Congress Cataloging-in-Publication Data

A CIP catalogue record for this book is
available from the Library of Congress.

British Library Cataloguing in Publication Data

A catalogue record for this book is
available from the British Library.

Printed in the United States on acid-free paper.

ISBN 978-0-85745-178-1 (pbk)

CONTENTS

INTRODUCTION
Migration, Development, and Social Transformation

Nina Glick Schiller and Thomas Faist

How should scholars interested in social analysis approach the topic of migration and development, and with what analytical tools, conceptual framework, or political stance? The topic of migration and development is becoming an important field of study, yet these questions are too rarely asked. In this volume, "Migration, Development, and Transnationalization: A Critical Stance," all six authors, each in his or her own way, and from various intellectual and disciplinary starting points, argue that the assumptions and paradigms underlying the study of the asymmetrical but mutual transfers of resources that accompany migration are deeply flawed and continue to reflect the interests of the global North, the most powerful states, and the globe-spanning institutions that serve their interests. The essays explore the role that contradictory discourses about migration are playing as modes of explanation for growing inequalities and an expanding global regime of militarized surveillance. Moreover, the essays provide useful alternative perspectives to the current received wisdom about the relationship between migration and development.

The approaches to the topic advocated in this volume both reflect and reflect on the current historical conjuncture. There has been a recent global financial downturn in which migrants, as Isotalo (this volume) points out, are among the most vulnerable. Yet migrants are seen as vital agents of international development by international financial institutions such as the World Bank, the European Union and its member states, international organizations from the United Nations, and a myriad of non-governmental organizations. For example, a United Nations Development Programme report, *Overcoming Barriers: Human Mobility and Development* (UNDP 2009: 3), argues that migrants "boost economic output, at little or no cost to locals. Indeed, there may be broader positive effects ... In migrants' countries of origin ... [m]oving generally brings benefits, most directly in the form of remittances sent to immediate family members. However, the benefits are also spread more broadly as remittances are spent—thereby generating jobs for local workers—and as behaviour changes in response to ideas from abroad. Women, in particular, may be liberated from traditional roles."

The new tendency of powerful financial and global governance institutions to highlight the positive agency of migrants and renew a discourse of migration and development followed the unleashing of neo-liberal market forces and the dramatic growth in economic and social disparities in many places in the world. In response, "[f]aced with the deepening asymmetries between developed and underdeveloped countries, the increase of social inequalities among national populaces, and a diversity of social conflicts, the promoters of neo-liberal globalization have resumed the discourse of development. Far from proposing structural and institutional changes, however, this just seeks to provide neo-liberalism with a 'human face'"

(Delgado Wise and Márquez Covarrubias, this volume; see also Faist, this volume). As the Washington Consensus fades, liberal rhetorics of democracy and freedom are increasingly and more openly accompanied or replaced by the use of military force and repression.

In this volume, Isotalo examines the relationships among mobility, discourses about human security, and the threat of terrorism, and Delgado Wise, Márquez Covarrubias, and Glick Schiller highlight migration in terms of the continuation of forms of imperialism. Placing the current revival of development narratives within an analysis of neo-liberalism and its discontents and contradictions helps the authors in this volume make sense of the anti-immigrant discourses and regulatory regimes that are concurrent with the celebration of migrants as agents of development. Glick Schiller and Isotalo address the resurgence of an interest in migration and development at a time when the movement of people, whether under the rubric of labor or of refugees, is increasingly restricted.

Scholars, political leaders, and policy makers have been discussing the relationship between migration and development for a long time, but with changing analytical tools, conceptual frameworks, political stances, and conclusions. At the beginning of the Industrial Revolution—with varying timing in different regions of Europe—political rulers tried to restrict workers from migrating across the borders of states. Passports were used to retain labor rather than to restrict its influx (Torpey 2000). In those cases, the links between migration and development were acknowledged, but the emphasis was on the ways in which migrants enriched the receiving state. The retention of labor was thought essential for the economic development and prosperity of the state of origin of the would-be migrants. On the other hand, the fact that the development of Europe depended on profits made from enslaved, indentured, and colonized migratory labor in other regions of the world has been too rarely acknowledged in European discourses about development. The wealth of the welfare state regimes that attract migrants to the North came in the past and continues to be built, in part, on migratory labor.

During the period of the African slave trade and European colonialism of the nineteenth and twentieth centuries, the development of the wealth and power of colonizing states was dependent on the controlled movement of labor in various colonies. At the end of the nineteenth century, as the academic disciplines became distinctive enterprises, separated from philosophy and theology, the conceptual frameworks for the discussion of migration and development also became more clearly articulated in ways that have continued to shape how we think about these fields.

First, there was a discursive shift from a concern with the mobility of people to a concern with the development of nation-states and thus also the control of flows across national borders. As Glick Schiller points out (this volume), the founders of geography, including Ratzell, initially approached migration without a national lens, concerned primarily about the relationship between the movement of people and the distribution of resources. However, Ratzell soon developed a political geography that located emotive power in the development, well-being, and expansion of the state. E. G. Ravenstein (1885), considered a founder of geography and migration studies, expounded "laws of migration," such as "migration increases as industries and commerce develop and transport improves" (ibid.: 178; cf. Ravenstein 1889). Ravenstein used British national data and raised questions about national development. Yet he was concerned with both internal and international migration, which allows for units of analysis such as rural/urban and rich/poor regions, thus differentiating his scholarship from the methodological nationalist orientation that characterizes much of recent migration scholarship.

By jettisoning methodological nationalism, an orientation that makes the nation-state the unit of analysis, scholars of migration and development are better able to examine differences of power within states and regions and around the globe. By not confining analyses within the borders of particular states, they can better explore the very uneven patterns of internal and international migration, remittance investment, class formations, knowledge, flows of capital, and infrastructure development. A critique of methodological nationalism does not start from a borderless or boundaryless world. Rather, it focuses on the very constitution of (state) borders and boundaries and their effect on the creation of inequalities between categories of persons within transnational processes of the production of wealth and various forms of power.

During the twentieth century, the social sciences became increasingly entwined not only with the nation-state as a unit of analysis but also with a concern for the well-being of a scholar's own national state. Migration scholars increasingly focused on the question of whether or not migration benefited the nation-state. They became concerned not only with economic development but also with the social cohesion of particular nation-states. Thus, they ignored the broader forces and legacies of colonialism and the processes of capital accumulation, concentration, and destruction that continually restructure industrial development, place, and the movements of people on a global scale. Despite a preoccupation with nation-state building, at the beginning of the twentieth century, migration scholars did initially acknowledge the transnational nature of the migration process. In their classic work, *The Polish Peasant in Europe and America*, William Thomas and Florian Znaniecki ([1918–1920] 1958) argued for strengthening what nowadays would be called the 'trans-national ties' of Polish migrants in the United States back to Poland by supporting agricultural cooperatives. By World War II, this transnational perspective on migration had been abandoned. Its recent resurgence and adoption by development scholars goes beyond the acknowledgment of mutual connections and influences to an argument that transnational ties inevitably produce win-win situations, that is, the benefits of transnational migration for both the sending and the receiving states.

This simplistic reading of migrants' transnationality has recently become apparent in migration and development scholarship, as can be seen in UNDP (2009). At the same time, most migration scholars based in the United States and Europe today portray migrants as a potential destabilizing force. They have revived past images of migrants as bearers of political (i.e., anarchistic, revolutionary), cultural, or religious difference. The language of difference once again globally encompasses those who move within discourses of securitization. Isotalo, for example, documents the resurgent politics of fear that increasingly equates human mobility and the flights from war, destruction, disaster, or economic collapse with terrorism.

Researchers who are critical of this perspective have repeatedly noted that the attribution of difference to the migrant foreigner has served to reinforce national identities, unities, and borders. As Fredrik Barth (1969) and a multitude scholars of identity have noted, borders and boundaries construct as well as mark cultural differences (Brubaker 2004; Sollors 1989). By taking a critical stance toward most migration and development narratives, the essays in this volume address the significance of portraying migrants as threats to the peace and security of nation-states, while simultaneously depicting them as heroic agents of development.

From the Migration-Development Mantra to the Migration-Development Nexus

Today, after years of low priority in academic and, above all, public debates, the link between migration and development has emerged again. Migration has mutated from being a problem for economic development to being a solution. In other words, the claim that development failure produces international migration has given way to the 'new mantra' that migration—that is, migrants—may help to advance economic development in their countries of origin (Kapur 2004). Thus, the traditional focus in migration studies on the causes and consequences of population movements has shifted to a focus on the types of migrants and migration that will promote development (for a detailed analysis, see Faist 2008). Hopes are pinned on labor migrants, especially temporary ones, sending financial remittances to their countries and locales of origin.

International organizations and governments of the Organisation for Economic Co-operation and Development (OECD) have renewed calls for schemes of temporary migration, presently referred to as 'circular migration'. These same authorities argue that the 'highly skilled' are transferring their expertise from North to South and from West to East ('brain gain'), rather than furthering the depletion of 'talent' in the South ('brain drain'). Discussions have focused both on individual persons who remit resources and on settled migrants in diasporas, who engage in collective financial remittances into selected development projects (e.g., infrastructure, health, education) and who facilitate 'social remittances', such as the transfer of human rights, gender equity, and democracy from North to South.

In short, certain policy circles in international agencies and state governments now maintain that facilitating certain types of population mobility will lead to development.

Generally, they argue that migrant remittances from receiving to sending countries could spur development in the long run. This view can be called, following a critical appraisal of such ideas, the 'migration-development mantra'. This viewpoint, however, is very different from the 'migration-development nexus'. It is important to note that the idea that migration and development are correlated and that economic development usually leads to more, rather than less, emigration—the insights of classical migration research into the migration-development nexus—is not equivalent to the notion that certain types of population mobility induce development, which is the claim made by policy makers and academics since the early 2000s.

Clearly, it is important to dig deeper and to connect this debate with the far-reaching societal changes and social transformations that are affecting both migration and development. We need to go beyond the current infatuation with the idea of international migration as a panacea for development. It helps to start with a simple observation, a foundational point that is made in the essays by Raúl Delgado Wise, Humberto Márquez Covarrubias, and Binod Khadria: the agenda for the migration-development mantra is firmly set by the countries in the North or West, while the supposed beneficiaries are the countries in the South or East.

The debate on migration and development that has emerged over the past half-dozen years is one of several to have occurred since the 1960s. In all cases, the policy and academic debates are overwhelmingly driven by Northern governments and have originated in international organizations such as the World Bank, which are governed by Northern majorities. In this asymmetric debate, it is important to point out that those in the South are not equals in setting principles and priorities. They are partners only in implementation.

That the Northern macro-agents set the agenda is obvious in various documents produced by institutions with global claims, such as the 2005 report of the Global Commission on International Migration. This report emphasizes not only the importance of financial remittances and ways to reduce transfer costs, but also the need for more highly skilled labor in OECD countries, and calls for new schemes of circular migration (GCIM 2005). Promoted by international organizations and Northern governments, the United Nations High-Level Dialogue on Migration and Development of 2006 was held "to discuss the multidimensional aspects of international migration and development in order to identify appropriate ways and means to maximize its development benefits and minimize its negative impacts."[1] By contrast, the governments of developing or transformation countries, such as the Philippines, no longer officially regard migration as a pillar of their formal development policy, if they ever did.

The new enthusiasm closely resembles that of the 1960s, when sending countries such as Turkey looked forward to receiving financial remittances, return migrants with Western work ethics, and the transfer of valuable skills. In the first regard, financial remittances now stand, as they did in the 1960s, at the core of hopes. Until the 2008 economic collapse, there had been a sharp increase in remittances over the past several years, up by almost 100 percent between 1999 and 2004, an amount at least twice as high as official development aid. Secondly, in the 1960s, migrants were supposed to transfer the right kind of work ethics 'back home'. Nowadays, migrants are also depicted as bearers of Western values, called 'social remittances', meaning that they are thought of as brokers for ideas such as gender equity and democratization. Thirdly, the 1960s concept that migrants were supposed to transfer skills has resurfaced within the concept of human capital.

Today's discussions differ only in the ever-increasing centrality of financial remittances, which have emerged as a form of securities market, and the focus on circular migration (Guarnizo 2003; Vertovec 2007). There is something for all agents involved who push the mantra. The World Bank (2006) focuses on individual remittances and thus also defines remittances as transfers by individuals, while development organizations tend to look at collective remittances by migrant associations, such as—at least in United States—the ubiquitous emphasis on hometown associations.

As Thomas Faist (this volume) points out, between the 1960s, when the argument that migration spurs development was prevalent, and today, there was an intervening period in which development experts claimed that the causality of the nexus ran in the opposite direction. Underdevelopment caused migration, and migration contributed to underdevelopment, especially through mechanisms such as brain drain. During much of the 1980s and part of the 1990s, the view prevailed that migration undermines the prospects for local economic development, resulting in a state of stagnation and dependency.

Arguing that the rapid growth of financial remittances to less-developed countries could help spur economic development, the World Bank (2002) initiated the latest support for migrants as agents of development. Subsequently, various development agents have projected the following additional benefits: (1) migrants will transfer both financial and social remittances; (2) the brain drain will gradually be replaced by a brain gain; (3) temporary (and circular) migration will stimulate development; (4) migrant diasporas will become development agents, in addition to individual migrants; and (5) economic development will eventually reduce emigration, although there will be an increase ('migration hump' or s-shaped migration curve) in the short and middle term. At present, the evidence for each and every one of these projected benefits is still very weak (Siddiqui 2005). For example, it all depends on whether remittances contribute to rising or declining income inequality.

In sharp contrast, Khadria, Delgado Wise, and Márquez Covarrubias (this volume) insist that any balanced view of the effects of migration must look not only at flows of resources from immigration countries back to emigration regions but also at flows running in the opposite direction. This would entail the much-debated brain drain, the costs of international migration, and the considerable expenses required in the attempt to obtain legal status in the immigration countries (Nolin 2006). As migration policies become increasingly and selectively restrictive, it stands to reason that irregular migrants have to invest ever more resources to legalize their status. This is one reason why claims that financial remittances have increased dramatically over the past decade have to be viewed cautiously. In sum, one would need to take a comprehensive look at the two-way flows of investment in migrants and remittances in order to gauge the economic potential of migrant transfers.

The Migration-Development Nexus and Social Transformation

Against this backdrop, the essays in this volume of *Critical Interventions* strive to focus on processes of social transformation in order to understand better and to contribute to the current round of discourse on the migration-development nexus. The authors step out of the debate, examine its foundational premises, find them flawed, and make suggestions to begin anew. They do not simply accompany their critique of the current state of affairs with calls for more research to confirm or refute or modify some of the assumptions listed above concerning the connection between migration and development, although this would also be a worthwhile task. Instead, given this state of affairs, "Migration, Development, and Transnationalization" approaches migration as an integral part of the processes of social transformation. Our authors take what Glick Schiller (this volume, forthcoming) has called a 'global perspective on migration'. This perspective, which offers a conceptual framework that includes inequalities between North and South, East and West, sees migrants as a major force in reshaping social and political formations.

The section opens with Nina Glick Schiller and Thomas Faist arguing specifically for such a global perspective. In "A Global Perspective on Migration and Development," Glick Schiller's focus is migration scholarship and the failure of scholars in this field to move beyond examinations of the role of migration in the development and social cohesion of specific nation-states. She calls attention to the failure of this scholarship to address the contradictory contemporary narratives that view migrants as agents of development but also as threats to the security and prosperity of nation-states.

Glick Schiller's global perspective on migration enables scholars to examine transnational fields of power within which migrant settlement and transnational connection occur in specific localities. This perspective does not deny the continuing role of nation-states of very different degrees of power in constituting a regulatory and surveillance regime that disciplines, restricts, and subordinates people trying to move within, as well as across, states. However, it allows for analytical space within which to examine the relationship between these states and broader globe-spanning networks of corporate and institutional power. To develop a global power perspective—which is an analytical stance, not a world systems or world society analysis—Glick Schiller argues that it is necessary to critique the methodological nationalism that has informed much of migration studies.

On the basis of this critique, Glick Schiller is able to note the emergence of a new global regime of labor exploitation that cannot be fully addressed within the rubric of migration and development. She warns that blithe descriptions and analysis of circulatory migration and transnational social connections that seem to be supportive of migrant mobility actually endorse a new global labor regime that denies rights and access to citizenship to most migrants. This regime, justified in the West through a defense of the 'welfare state', which dismisses the humanity of the migrant sector of the workforce, is corrosive to the aspirations for social and economic justice of citizens and non-citizens alike. However, exactly because the new endorsement of a transnational temporary labor regime is so contradictory, Glick Schiller suggests that the shared threats to human freedom it contains provide new bases for global perspectives on migration and common struggles for social transformation.

Thomas Faist's essay, "Transnationalization and Development: Toward an Alternative Agenda," enters the discussion through a critical examination of the ways in which development studies have approached migration. He notes that migration and development discourses generally take the global South as the object of development, obscuring the transnational flows of labor and capital to the North, which serve to develop that region. Adopting the historical perspective that the authors of this volume share, he reviews previous moments at which migration was said to be key to the development of the South. This allows him to note how the current resurrection of migration as an agent of development is marked by the transnationalization of the model, with mobile people emerging as central agents of social transformation.

As does Glick Schiller, Faist reflexively asks, why now? Why have certain understandings of migration and development emerged at this particular historical conjuncture? Taking note of the intense contemporary interlinkages that are signaled by terms such as 'globalization', Faist suggests that an analysis of the actual contemporary relationships of power is needed, and this requires an alternative perspective on social transformation that cannot be contained within discussions of migration and development. He identifies the changing discourses on market, state and community, and the geo-political power structure as promising points of departure. Faist looks to an analysis of transnational social formations and places the possibility and limitations of migrants' agency within that framework.

Riina Isotalo begins her query into the current prominence of the topic of migration and development by speaking of the politicization of transnationalization. In her essay, "Politicizing the Transnational: On Implications for Migrants, Refugees, and Scholarship," she notes that despite the fact that the initial scholarship on transnational migration was offered within a critique of uneven globalization, the paradigm has been taken up within current efforts to depict all human mobility as a threat to global and national security and as a prop for the faltering logic of neo-liberal free market development. Isotalo argues that the "developmentalization of mobility is not merely a consequence of the contemporary forces of capitalist restructuring but is as much related to the securitization of mobility."

In keeping with the emphasis of this volume on the historical contextualizing of social theory, Isotalo traces the way in which refugees have been configured in terms of security and economic development at various points in the twentieth century and up to the present time. Her essay calls attention to the fact that "migration is now a part of security policies" (see also Faist 2003), a point only peripherally addressed by most migration scholars, who are caught up in discussions of migration integration and social cohesion within their own nation-states. The end result is that when the European Union talks about a "global approach on migration," the term 'global' is not deployed in the same way that Glick Schiller and other authors in this volume use it. While this book speaks of 'the global' to address globe-spanning and locally constituting political and economic processes, imperial ambitions and projects, and social movements, both powerful Northern institutions, such as the European Union, and many migration scholars limit their global discussions primarily to remittance transfers for development needs and to security concerns linked to refugee flows across borders.

The question of the unit of analysis is central to Isotalo's approach to the politicization of both migrants' transnational connections and the development policies that highlight them. Isotalo notes that development and security discourses indulge in a form of "methodological individualism" in which individual migrants are highlighted as objects of scrutiny and as sources of remittances. This means that the broader social forces and institutional structures of power that have created the structural adjustment and neo-liberal environment and its instabilities—the forces that are highlighted by the authors of this volume—disappear from the analytic frame. Migrants fleeing from the so-called new wars that are produced by these instabilities are used as an "indicator of the lack of security." Containing migration then becomes key to ensuring security, and "migration management … [becomes] a strategic matter of top priority in the European Union." In adopting a global perspective on migration, Isotalo provides an innovative approach to the current discussion of remittances and development. She illustrates her argument by suggesting that the ways in which Palestinian rights are configured or denied in various areas of the Middle East shed light on more general approaches to the control of refugee flows, development, and security.

Raúl Delgado Wise and Humberto Márquez Covarrubias underscore Glick Schiller's and Faist's argument that any discussion of migration and development must begin by exploring the assumptions and units of analysis that underlie the project. In their essay, "Understanding the Relationship between Migration and Development: Toward a New Theoretical Approach," they situate their critique of contemporary migration and development discourses within a clearly articulated political economy of development, a perspective that they believe is generally lacking in migration scholarship. In offering this analytical stance, Delgado Wise and Márquez Covarrubias creatively build upon the work done within the last 40 years to develop and critique dependency theory, world-systems theory, and the political economy of neo-liberal globalization (England and Ward 2007; Frank 1969; Harvey 2005; Marini 1973; Rhodes 1970; Wallerstein 1979).

Delgado Wise and Márquez Covarrubias argue that discussions of migration and development must begin by acknowledging the inequalities that underlie migration flows. Noting the relationship between migration and efforts to restructure capital globally in line with neo-liberal agendas, they point out that the "great paradox of the migration-development agenda is that it leaves the principles that underpin neo-liberal globalization intact and does not affect the specific way in which neo-liberal policies are applied in migrant-sending countries." In centering their interest on migrant-sending countries, they offer a view from outside of North America and the European Union that is generally under-represented in migration and development discourse. As they point out, scholars in those regions, such as Bambirra (1978), Cardoso and Faletto (1969), Dos Santos (1974), Frank (1969), Furtado (1969), and Marini (1973), had stepped out of a methodological nationalist framing and utilized analyses of transnational processes to explain underdevelopment long before this critique emerged in the developed North.

From this stance, Delgado Wise and Márquez Covarrubias also are able to place migrant agency within broader social movements for transformation, offering not only a critique of the existing paradigm but an alternative framework and a vision of a means to facilitate the struggle for social and economic justice and equality. Rather than proffering a grand, homogenizing economic reductionist narrative, their framework examines the cultural power of dominant narratives, the specificity of regional arrangements, the dynamics and interpenetration between various geographic scales, and "a notion of development that surpasses the limitations of normative and decontextualized concepts and takes into account the necessary role of social transformation (i.e., structural, strategic, and institutional changes) in the improvement of living conditions among the general population."

In his essay, "Adversary Analysis and the Quest for Global Development: Optimizing the Dynamic Conflict of Interest in the Transnational Divide of Migration," Binod Khadria confronts the win-win narratives with a view from the South. That positionality, developed over the course of centuries of colonial and neo-colonial inequalities, facilitates his queries into the relationship between the unequal economic, military, political, and cultural power of the North and the ways in which discourses about migration and development are framed. Khadria deconstructs the illusions about the equality of power between sending and receiving states by positioning them as adversaries. He calls for a dynamic understanding of the stakes and the stake-holders in the contemporary relationship between transnational processes including migration and the hierarchies of wealth and power between and within world regions and states. As is the case with the other authors in this volume, he asks global questions. Khadria wants to know what discussions of development would actually look like if we thought of the well-being of people around the world.

In pursuit of answers to these questions, Khadria refutes the widely made claims that the South benefits from return workers with enhanced skills, remittances, and technology transfers. He contrasts claims of benefits to the facts on the ground, such as those of patent regimes that tilt the flow of profits to the North when technology is adopted by the South. Rejecting the language of mutual benefit, Khadria begins a discussion of migration and development by acknowledging the adversarial relationship that exists between the regions. He argues that only when the actual situation is acknowledged, by taking the perspective of the other side into consideration, will it be possible to find common ground from which mutual good might be organized.

Conclusion

There is no doubt that, in principle, migration can produce outcomes that are beneficial to receiving countries, which attract 'global talent' by competing for the 'best and brightest' and which are also dependent on unskilled labor from abroad. These outcomes can be likewise beneficial to sending countries and the migrating populations, with their different class backgrounds and interests. Yet the conditions for realizing these benefits are complex because they are linked to transformations in the fundamental balance of power between regions and states and within states. Consequently, we view strategies that tout remittance-led development as being at best naive. This is so because migration alone cannot remove structural constraints to economic growth and greater democracy (Glick Schiller and Fouron 2001). The essays in this volume collectively emphasize the need for a many-pronged development strategy, in which the potential benefits of migration are small parts of larger plans to reduce inequality and to improve economic infrastructure, social welfare, and political governance.

In short, this book, "Migration, Development, and Transnationalization: A Critical Stance," brings together a series of essays on migration and development that takes scholars and development practitioners beyond the blinders of the bulk of current migration and development theory and practice. We challenge those who are searching for ways to address the morass of development failure, vitriolic attacks on immigrants, or sanguine views about migrant agency to put aside their methodological nationalism and pursue alternative pathways into the topic that can lead us out of the quagmire of poverty, violence, and fear that seems to be enveloping the globe.

Acknowledgments

We would like to thank the Center for Interdisciplinary Research (ZiF, Zentrum für interdisziplinäre Forschung) at Bielefeld University, which sponsored the ZiF Cooperation Group, "Transnationalization and Development(s): Concepts and Venues for Research." Earlier versions of most contributions were presented and discussed in workshops of this group.

Notes

1. See http://www.un.org/esa/population/migration/hld/index.html.

References

Bambirra, Vania. 1978. *Teoría de la dependencia: Una anticrítica.* Mexico City: Ediciones Era.

Barth, Fredrik, ed. 1969. *Ethnic Groups and Boundaries: The Social Organization of Culture Difference.* Boston: Little Brown.

Brubaker, Rogers. 2004. *Ethnicity without Groups.* Cambridge, MA: Harvard University Press.

Cardoso, Fernando H., and Enzo Faletto. 1969. *Dependencia y desarrollo en America Latina.* Mexico City: Siglo XXI.

Dos Santos, Theotonio. 1974. *Dependencia y cambio social.* Buenos Aires: Amorrortu.

England, Kim, and Kevin Ward, eds. 2007. *Neoliberalization: States, Networks, Peoples.* Malden, MA: Blackwell.

Faist, Thomas. 2003. "Extension du domaine de la lutte: International Migration and Security." *International Migration Review* 36, no. 1: 7–14.

_____. 2008. "Migrants as Transnational Development Agents: An Inquiry into the Newest Round of the Migration-Development Nexus." *Population, Space and Place* 14, no. 1: 21–42.

Frank, Andre Gunder. 1969. *Latin America: Underdevelopment or Revolution.* New York: Monthly Review Press.

Furtado, Celso. 1969. *Desarrollo y subdesarrollo.* Buenos Aires: Editorial Universitaria.

GCIM (Global Commission on International Migration). 2005. *Migration in an Interconnected World: New Directions for Action.* http://www.gcim.org/attachements/gcim-complete-report-2005.pdf.

Glick Schiller, Nina. Forthcoming. "A Global Perspective on Transnational Migration: Migration without Methodological Nationalism." In *Diaspora and Transnationalism: Concepts, Theories and Methods,* ed. Rainer Bauböck and Thomas Faist. Amsterdam: University of Amsterdam and IMISCOE.

Glick Schiller, Nina, and Georges Fouron. 2001. *Georges Woke Up Laughing: Long-Distance Nationalism and the Search for Home.* Durham, NC: Duke University Press.

Guarnizo, Louis. 2003. "The Economics of Transnational Living." *International Migration Review* 37, no. 3: 666–699.

Harvey, David. 2005. *A Brief History of Neoliberalism.* New York: Oxford University Press.

Kapur, Devesh. 2004. "Remittances: The New Development Mantra?" G-24 Discussion Paper Series, No. 29. Washington, DC: World Bank.

Marini, Ruy Mauro. 1973. *Dialéctica de la dependencia.* Mexico City: Ediciones Era.

Nolin, Catherine. 2006. *Transnational Ruptures: Gender and Forced Migration.* Aldershot: Ashgate.

Ravenstein, Ernest G. 1885. "The Laws of Migration." *Journal of the Royal Statistical Society* 48: 167–235.

_____. 1889. "The Laws of Migration: Second Paper." *Journal of the Royal Statistical Society* 52: 241–305.

Rhodes, Robert, ed. 1970. *Imperialism and Underdevelopment: A Reader.* New York: Monthly Review Press.

Siddiqui, Tasneem, ed. 2005. *Migration and Development: Pro-Poor Policy Choices.* Dhaka: University Press. Published in association with Great Britian's Department for International Development and Refugee and Migratory Movements Research Unit.

Sollors, Werner, ed. 1989. *The Invention of Ethnicity.* New York: Oxford University Press.

Thomas, William, and Florian Znaniecki. [1918–1920] 1958. *The Polish Peasant in Europe and America.* New York: Dover.

Torpey, John. 2000. *The Invention of the Passport: Surveillance, Citizenship and the State.* Cambridge: Cambridge University Press.

UNDP (United Nations Development Programme). 2009. *Overcoming Barriers: Human Mobility and Development.* http://hdr.undp.org/en/media/HDR_2009_EN_Complete.pdf.

Vertovec, Steven. 2007. "Circular Migration: The Way Forward in Global Policy?" Working Papers #4, International Migration Institute, Oxford University. http://www.imi.ox.ac.uk/pdfs/wp4-circular-migration-policy.pdf.

Wallerstein, Immanuel. 1979. *The Capitalist World-Economy.* Cambridge: Cambridge University Press.

World Bank. 2002. *Globalization, Growth, and Poverty.* Washington, DC: World Bank.

_____. 2006. *Global Economic Prospects 2006: Economic Implications of Remittances and Migration.* Washington, DC: World Bank.

A GLOBAL PERSPECTIVE ON MIGRATION AND DEVELOPMENT

Nina Glick Schiller

On a phone booth in Manchester, England—where I now live as a transmigrant—I saw an advertisement that read "Send money home from closer to home." It went on to announce that you can now send funds to locations around the world from any British Post Office. The Post Office, whose sales operations have now been privatized, has joined businesses around the world that seek to profit from migrant remittances. Spanish banks extend mortgages to migrants living in Spain who are building houses 'back home' in Ecuador and elsewhere in Latin America, while appliances stores in Brazil process orders for customers whose source of payment comes from family members living abroad (Lapper 2007a). Migrants' money transfers, purchases of costly commodities, and homeland investments figure large in the recent policies of powerful globe-spanning financial institutions, such as the World Bank, which have proclaimed migrant remitters as the new agents of international development (de Haas 2007; Fajnzylber and López 2008; Lapper 2007b; World Bank 2006). Meanwhile, researchers of development and migration, while noting the possibilities and contradictions of migrant remittances on sending and receiving localities, take for granted that migrants are both local and transnational actors (Dannecker 2007; Faist 2008; Fauser 2007; Guarnizo 2007; Østergaard-Nielsen 2007; Preis 2007; Raghuram 2007).

Yet at the same time that the transnationality of migrants is being both routinely documented and celebrated, politicians and the mass media in Europe and the United States are focusing their concern primarily on questions of 'integration', portraying migrants' transnational ties as threats to 'national security.' In these discourses, migrants are attacked for their supposed lack of loyalty to their new homeland. Politicians, demagogic leaders, and media personalities blame migrants for national economic problems, including the growing disparity between rich and poor, the shrinking of the middle class, the reduction in the quality and availability of public services and education, and the rising costs of health care and housing. Calls for tightening borders and ending the influx of migrants are widespread, and countries around the world are shutting their doors in the faces of people desperately trying to flee war, rape, and pillage. In the meantime, rates of deportation are rising dramatically.

Within these anti-migration discourses, little is said about migrants' provision of vital labor, services, and skills to their new land or their role in the reproduction of workforces—including their sustenance, housing, education, and training—in countries around the world. It is true that there is some appreciation for one current in the migrant stream. States as diverse as Singapore and Germany welcome 'global talent' in the form of professional and highly skilled immigrants. Yet this differentiation only serves to reinforce the viewpoint that most migrants are undesirable and that migration should cease.

What is the response of migration theorists to the present contradictory positions on migration whereby migrant remittances are defined as a vital resource, and yet those who send remittances are castigated and increasingly denied the right to move across borders? To date, I would argue, migration scholars have not established a critical perspective that can adequately make sense of the contradictions. They have not developed a global perspective that can place within the same analytical framework debates about international migration and development, national rhetorics on migration and refugee policies, and migration scholarship. Instead, migration scholars have adopted the perspective of their respective nation-states.

Much of the European and US scholarship on migration confines itself to questions such as 'how well do they fit into our society', 'what are the barriers that keep them from fully joining us', or 'which cultures or religions do not fit in?' In the United States, migration scholars who see themselves as pro-immigration increasingly embrace what I call 'born-again assimilationism' to show that migrants do indeed become part of the national fabric and contribute to it (R. Smith 2006; Waldinger and Fitzgerald 2004). New assimilationists and integrationists distinguish themselves from the old by updating what they mean by immigrants becoming an integral part of their new society (Alba and Nee 2003; Heckmann 2003; Joppke and Morawska 2002; Morawska 2003). Although these scholars accept the persistence of ethnic identities, home ties, and transnational networks as in some cases compatible with integration, they continue to see migration as a potential threat to the nation-state. They believe that international migration warrants investigation because it is fundamentally problematic for the social cohesion of the 'host society'. For example, Michael Bommes and Andrew Geddes (2000: 6) are concerned that "migration can be taken as part of a process that erodes the classical arrangement by which welfare states provide an ordered life course for the members of the national community, i.e., for their citizens in exchange for political loyalty." As Bommes (2005) has noted, "assimilationists conceptualise ... society as a big national collective." In Europe, the term used is 'integration', which is often differentiated from assimilation (Esser 2003, 2006). However, whether the concept being deployed is integration or assimilation, most scholars of migration reflect and contribute to an approach to the nation-state that depicts a nation and its migrants as fundamentally and essentially distinct—both socially and culturally.[1]

It is likely that future scholars will demonstrate that the revival of the assimilationist theory and the 'new' integrationism at the beginning of the twenty-first century, rather than representing an advance in social science, reflected the neo-liberal project of the restructuring of nation-states. Rescaled but not replaced in relation to regional and global reorganizations of economic and political power, nation-states began, as they did at the turn of the twentieth century, and with the assistance of migration scholars, to build national identities at the expense of immigrants. Even scholars of transnational migration, including those who highlight the role of migrants in transnational development projects, are now concluding their articles with reassurances that migrants' transnational activities are relatively minimal or contribute to their integration into the nation-state in which they have settled (Guarnizo, Portes, and Haller 2003; R. Smith 2006). They have not provided a perspective on migration that explains why major global financial institutions, which portray migrants as agents of development through remittances that sustain impoverished communities, seem unconcerned that these very same people are increasingly disdained and excluded in their countries of settlement.

In this essay, I build on scholars who advocate an institutional analysis of contemporary migration policies and discourses, but I continue the argument further by proposing a 'global power perspective' that can link contemporary forces of capitalist restructuring to the specific localities within which migrants live and struggle. After a postmodern period in which any attempt to use or develop globe-spanning perspectives was dismissed as a 'grand narrative', scholars in an array of disciplines, and with very different politics, have once again tried to connect the local and particular with an analysis of broader forces. Contemporary globe-spanning trends have been approached as globalization (Mittleman 1996), network society (Castells 1996), and empire (Hardt and Negri 2000). Yet, ironically, many migration scholars who study cross-border population movements remain inured to concepts of society and culture that reflect historic nation-state building projects. These projects obscure the past and contemporary transnational fields of power that shape political and economic development.

A global power perspective on migration could facilitate the description of social processes by introducing units of analysis and research paradigms that are not built on the methodological nationalism of much migration discourse. It would allow researchers to make sense of local variation and history in relation to transnational processes and connections. Such a framework would allow us to identify contradictions and disjunctures in contemporary scholarship, as well as forms, spaces, ideologies, and identities of resistance to oppressive and global relations of unequal power.

One essay cannot, of course, do more than outline such an alternative analytic framework. In sketching a different approach to migration and development that builds on a global power perspective, this essay briefly (1) critiques methodological nationalism; (2) addresses neoliberal restructuring of localities of migrant settlement and ongoing connection; (3) situates the topic of remittances within transnational social fields of uneven power; and (4) analyzes the countervailing hegemonic processes that are encapsulated in state migration policies and development discourses.

I want to be clear from the very beginning that by eschewing methodological nationalism and establishing a global framework for the study of migrant settlement and transnational connection, I am not saying—and have never argued—that the nation-state is withering away.[2] I am asserting that to understand the restructuring of globe-spanning institutional arrangements, including the changing role and continuing significance of states, we need a perspective that is not constrained by the borders of the nation-state. This is because nation-states are positioned and transformed within global fields of power, and consequently these fields affect the migration process, including movement, settlement, and transnational connection. At the same time, through their connections between places and their actions that affect places, migrants are active agents of contemporary transformations on local, national, and global scales. My particular interest is the way in which migrants' settlement and transnational connections both shape and are shaped by the contemporary restructuring of capital and the scalar repositioning of specific localities (Glick Schiller, Caglar, and Guldbrandsen 2006).

Tracing the Lineages of Methodological Nationalism in Migration Scholarship

A growing number of social theorists have argued that methodological nationalism has been central to much of Western social science (Beck 2000; Martins 1974; A. Smith

1983; Wimmer and Glick Schiller 2002a, 2002b). Methodological nationalism is an ideological orientation that
approaches the study of social and historical processes
as if they were contained within the borders of individual
nation-states. Nation-states are conflated with societies,
and the members of those states are assumed to share a
common history and set of values, norms, social customs,
and institutions. Some writers label this orientation the
'container' theory of society to highlight that most social
theorists, including Emile Durkheim, Max Weber, and
Talcott Parsons, have contained their concept of society
within the territorial and institutional boundaries of the
nation-state (Basch, Glick Schiller, and Szanton Blanc
1994; Urry 2000; Wolf 1982). A methodological nationalist perspective in migration scholarship led to the separation of development studies from the study of immigrant
incorporation into a new country. To reject methodological nationalism requires migration scholars to recover
an approach to migration that does not use nation-states
as units of analysis but rather studies the movement of
people across space in relationship to forces that structure
political economy. These forces include states but are
not confined to states and their policies. Furthermore,
national and international policies are considered within
the same analytical lens (Nye 1976).

I am calling for scholars to recover rather than develop
a global perspective on migration, since aspects of this
approach were widespread during the period of globalization that took place from the 1880s to the 1920s. At that
time, there was broad interest in the diffusion of ideas and
material culture through the migration of people. Scholars
such as Friedrich Ratzel (1882) treated all movements of
people over the terrain as a single phenomenon linked to
the distribution of resources across space. Ratzel's writing
reflected the assumptions of his times, namely, that the

movements of people were normal and natural. The fact that migrants came and went and maintained their ties to home by sending back money to buy land, initiate businesses, and support families and village projects—all this was understood as a typical aspect of migration. Workers migrated into regions in which there was industrial development and returned home or went elsewhere when times were bad. England, Germany, Switzerland, France, the United States, Brazil, and Argentina built industrialized economies with the help of millions of migrant labors, who worked in factories, fields, mills, and mines. In general, during that era of globalization and imperial penetration, most European countries abolished the passport and visa system that they had installed in the first half of the nineteenth century (Torpey 2000). The United States did not restrict migration from Europe and required neither passports nor visas.[3]

This period of unequal globalization was shaped by fierce competition among many states for control of far-reaching transnational commercial networks. The wealth and workforce of many nations were produced elsewhere, and colonial projects were the basis of the accumulation of nationally based capital. Governmental regimes increasingly deployed the concepts of nation, national unity, and national economy in ways that obscured the transnational basis of their nation-state building projects. The people who lived in these states faced increasing pressure to use a single national language, to identify with a national history, to understand their practices and beliefs to be part of a national culture, to equate concepts of blood and nation, and to be willing to sacrifice their lives for the nation's honor.

Both international migrants and citizens of migrant-receiving states sought explanations for the rapid changes they were experiencing. Political theories and social movements that could speak to global transformations flourished, including international socialism, anarchism, pan-Africanism, feminism, nationalism, scientific racism, and anti-imperialism (Bodnar 1985; Gabaccia and Ottanelli 2001; Gilroy 1992; Potts 1990; van Holthoon and van der Linden 1988). However, state officials, politicians, and intellectuals supported nationalist ideologies that portrayed individuals as having only one country and one identity. In so doing, they contributed to the view that immigrants embodied cultural, physical, and moral characteristics that differentiated them from their host society and therefore merited study. It was at that moment—and in conjunction with the mounting pressure to delineate national borders more firmly by closing them—that a scholarship of immigrant settlement became delineated. The transnational social fields of migrants and their engagement in internationalism and other forms of non-state-based social movements increasingly were seen as problematic and finally disappeared from view. The study of migration was divided between demographers and geographers, who studied movement between nation-states, and sociologists, who studied settlement and assimilation.

As a result of that moment, several complementary but differentiated logics were deployed: (1) the sociology of migration was situated exclusively within national territories; (2) the notion of national origin was racialized through the popularization of the concept of national stocks; (3) assimilationist theory was developed within the hegemonic narrative of race and nation; and (4) national stocks came to be seen as differentiated by culture and were designated either as 'nationalities' or as 'national minorities' who resided within a state of settlement. Current scholarship on migrant incorporation and transnational connection continues to be shaped not only by these past approaches but also by the current historical conjuncture in which the leaders of migrant-receiving states are emotively legitimating national discourses and narratives.

Today, the 'ethnic group' continues to serve as the primary unit of analysis with which to study and interpret migration settlement, transnational migration, and diaspora. Often termed 'communities,' the ethnic group has become the bedrock of studies of migrant settlement. This remains true despite a voluminous historical and ethnographic literature that (1) identifies the constructed nature of ethnic identities and ethnic group boundaries, (2) includes detailed ethnographies of institutional processes through which ethnic categories and identities are constructed and naturalized by local and transnational actors, and (3) provides copious accounts of divisions based on class, religion, region of origin, and politics among the members of the supposedly 'same' group (Barth 1969; Brubaker 2004; Caglar 1990, 1997; Glick Schiller 1977, 1999; Glick Schiller et al. 1987; Gonzalez 1988; Kastoryano 2002; Sollors 1989). The use of ethnic groups as units of analysis is a logical but unacceptable consequence of the methodological nationalism of mainstream migration studies.

The problematic framing of migration research in terms of ethnic groups within nation-states obscures the effects of the global restructuring of capital on the population, both migrant and non-migrant, in a specific locality. Even studies of migrants' transnational connections that seemed to offer an analytical perspective beyond the nation-state have tended to examine specific ethnic trajectories and have said little about the ways in which the restructuring of economic, political, and social capital affects specific forms of migrant settlement and transnational connections. Few researchers have noted the significance of locality in shaping migrants' transnational social and economic fields.[4]

In short, the methodological nationalism of many migration scholars, reflecting the entanglements of disciplinary histories with nation-state building projects, precludes them from accurately describing the transnational social fields of unequal power that are integral to the migrant experience. Because their scholarship is built on units of analysis that developed within nation-state building projects, few migration scholars situate national terrains and discourses within an analysis of the restructuring of the global economy, the rescaling of cities, and the rationalization of a resurgent imperialist agenda.[5]

Addressing the Neo-liberal Restructuring of Localities of Migrant Settlement and Ongoing Connection

Working within a Marxist framework, David Harvey (2003, 2005) and a number of geographers have emphasized that while one can talk about the intensification of global processes of capital flow and flexible accumulation, capital reproduction always comes to ground somewhere. Since capital is ultimately a social relationship, when it is reconstituted in a specific place, the process destroys previously emplaced social relationships and the infrastructures and environments in which they were situated and constructs others. Although differentiated in terms of the path-dependent trajectories of a specific place, the effects of the restructuring of capital are not confined to only one place; rather, the transformation of one place affects many others. The reconstitution of capital disrupts previous arrangements of power and structures new relationships of production, reproduction of labor, distribution, and consumption that extend into other localities.

The processes of the creation and destruction of capital—as it represents the concentration of relationships of production within time and space—is an ongoing feature of capitalism. However, beginning in the 1970s, this general process was reconfigured on a global scale through the uneven and disparate implementation of a series of initiatives widely known as the 'neo-liberal agenda'. Neo-liberalism can be defined as a series of projects of capital accumulation that have reconstituted social relations of production in ways that dramatically curtail state investment in public activities, resulting in the reduction of state services and benefits and the diversion of public monies and resources to develop private service-oriented industries from health care to housing (sometimes in arrangements termed 'public-private partnerships'). At the same time, the neo-liberal project also relentlessly pushes toward global production through the elimination of state intervention in a host of economic issues—from tariffs to workers' rights—including the organization of labor, space, state institutions, military power, governance, membership, and sovereignty (Harvey 2005; Jessop 2003). Neo-liberalism has allowed for the creation of wealth by destroying and replacing previous relations of production, consumption, and distribution and by generating new forms of desire. These transformations have affected the quality of life of migrants and natives alike.

Neo-liberal projects take the form of specific sets of ideas and policies that may or may not be successfully implemented. These ideas are held, shaped, defended, and contested by a range of actors, including social scientists, whether or not they are directly linked to policy. The broader projects involve not just the domain of economics but also politics, cultural practices, ideas about self and society, and the production and dissemination of images and narratives. Neo-liberal plans are implemented on the ground and differentially, depending not just on different national policies but also on specific local histories, including that of migration.

The work of geographers on the neo-liberal restructuring of capital and space highlights the various mechanisms that require all places to compete for investments in new economies (Brenner 2004; N. Smith 1995). All of the resources that cities have, including their human resources, which encompass the migrants and their skills and qualities, acquire a new value and become assets in this competition. Migrants are not only part of the new, just-in-time sweatshop industries that accompany the restructuring of some cities. They provide highly skilled labor that also contributes to the human capital profile of various cities. The 'cultural diversity' of migrants is an important factor in the competitive struggle between the cities. Beyond the marketing of ethnic culture, migrants contribute to the cultural industries of the cities in which they are settling, from media to cuisine, fashion, and graphic design (Caglar 2005, 2007; Scott 2004; Zukin 1995). The place and role of migrants in this competition might differ, depending on the scalar positioning of these cities.

The implementation of neo-liberal agendas had disrupted fixed notions of nested, territorially bounded units of city, region, state, and globe. The scholarship on neo-liberalism documents the ways in which all localities have become global in that none are delimited only by the regulatory regime and economic processes of the state in which they are territorially based. The state itself is rescaled to play new roles by channeling flows of relatively unregulated capital and participating in the constitution of global regulatory regimes enforced by the World Trade Organization (WTO) and international financial institutions. To emphasize the processual, competitive, and political aspects of the spatial restructuring of capital, some geographers speak of 'rescaling'. They note that when localities change the parameters of their global, national, and/ or regional connectedness and lines of power that serve to govern territory, they in effect 'jump scale' (Swynge-douw 1997). Rather than understanding the local and global scale as either discrete levels of social activities or hierarchical analytical abstractions, as in previous geographies of space, "the global and the local (as well as the national) are [understood to be] mutually constitutive" (Brenner 2001: 134–135). Localities do, however, differ in their positioning in terms of globe-spanning hierarchies of economic and political power.

The scalar positioning of a locality—its success in competing for investments, a range of industries, and businesses services and in attracting highly skilled new economy workers—shapes the incorporation, if differentially, of all residents of that locality. Hence, the research framework I am suggesting—what I call a 'locality analysis' of a global power paradigm—places migrants and natives in the same conceptual framework. Locality analysis turns our attention to the relationships that develop between the residents of a place and institutions that are situated locally, regionally, nationally, and globally, without making prior assumptions about how these relationships are shaped by ethnicity, nationality, or national territory. All of these factors and others that affect opportunity structures remain a matter of investigation.

Although scale theorists have said almost nothing about migrant incorporation, it is evident that a locality analysis built on that scholarship provides important theoretical openings with which to approach the significance of locality in migrant incorporation. The relative positioning of a place within hierarchical fields of power may well lay the ground for the life chances and incorporation opportunities of migrants and those who are native to the place. In order to understand the different modes and dynamics of both migrant and transnational incorporation, we need to address the broader rescaling processes affecting the

cities in which migrants are settling. A scalar perspective
can bring into this discussion the missing spatial aspects
of socio-economic power, which is exercised differently
in various localities. The concept of scalar positioning
also introduces socio-spatial parameters to the analysis
of' locality in migration scholarship (Glick Schiller and
Caglar 2009, 2010).

For students of migration, this perspective reminds us
that migrants, as part of the processes of capital reproduction, are agents of the reshaping of localities. Migrants
become part of the restructuring of the social fabric of the
several localities to which they may be connected through
their transnational networks and become actors within
new forms of governing territory. Of course, migrants'
roles in each place are themselves shaped in the context
of rescaling processes themselves. At the same time, pathways of migrant settlement are shaped by the opportunity
structures and restrictions of particular places, including the type of labor needed and the way that labor is
recruited and organized within those places.

It is through making this type of locality analysis that
we can assess the variety of ways that migrants contribute
to the opportunity structures of various locations and the
degree to which they become one of several factors in the
restructuring of a place. This places the migrants as actors
within larger global forces and moves our discussion
beyond the limitations of a model of migration, development, and remittances. Some of the roles that migrants
play as agents of global restructuring are described in the
transnational migration literature but are not sufficiently
analyzed within broader processes of capital development and destruction. Other migrant contributions are
rarely acknowledged because they are not clearly visible
through an ethnic lens. My list of forms in which migrants
serve as agents of restructuring and rescaling includes

their role in contributing to the rise of property values, gentrifying neighborhoods, creating new industries or businesses, developing new trade connections and patterns of marketing and distribution, and changing patterns of consumption.

Contingent on the positioning of a place globally, migrants make different kinds of contributions, which, depending on the stance of the observer, may be judged good or bad. Take, for example, the role of migrants as gentrifiers both in their place of settlement and in localities to which they are transnationally connected. In cites of settlement, which are in the process of successful restructuring, migrants may contribute to the reinvention of urban neighborhoods previously considered undesirable by buying property in particular localities where property values have been low (Goode 2010; Salzbrunn 2010). Migrants may be well placed to buy property because they are able to draw on family credit or pooled resources to invest in and improve the housing stock or local neighborhood businesses (Glick Schiller, Caglar, and Guldbrandsen 2006). Thus, migrants may stabilize, restore, or gentrify neighborhoods and may even contribute to the global marketing of a city. Migrant investments in housing and property may transform neighborhoods within their transnational social field in ways that increase economic opportunities or economic disparities between localities.

As I have argued elsewhere (Glick Schiller and Caglar 2009, 2010), migration scholarship's binary division of foreigner and natives, which is legitimated through the adoption of the nation-state as the unit of both study and analysis, leaves no conceptual space to address questions of the global restructuring of region and locality that serves as the nexus of migrant incorporation and transnational connection and to which migrants contribute in ways that may rescale cities. Except for global cities theory, the insightful and powerful social theorizing of locality and scale produced by urban geographers has not entered into either migration theory or discussions about migration and development. To note that migrant departure, settlement, and transnational connections are shaped by the positioning of localities and regions within globally structured hierarchies of economic and political power would disrupt the homogenization of the national terrain that is imposed by migration theory and echoed in development discourses.

Placing Remittance Flows within Transnational Social Fields of Uneven Power

A transnational social field is a complex of networks that connects people across the borders of nation-states and to specific localities (Glick Schiller 2003, 2006). Here I use the term 'social field' to refer not to a metaphoric space but to a set of social relations, unequal in terms of the power of the various actors, through which people live their lives. Migrants who send remittances may reconfigure social relations as part and parcel of the transnational processes that reconstitute localities. These localities may be home-towns, but migrants may also choose to invest in property and businesses in capital or key cities that were not their places of origin. Migrants' labor, cultural and social capital, and agency contribute to the positioning of localities within unequal transnational relationships of power.

Migration processes cannot be seen as a *sui generis* activity with an internal dynamic that can be studied in its own right, without reference to the global-local interface of the reconstitution of capital. This is not to deny that one can track the development of an internal logic within a migration stream, as Douglas Massey (Massey et al. 1998) has done so well in his research on Mexican migration. As migration takes on its own logic with transnational networks, a specific migration trajectory and the networks that connect places become part and parcel of the restructuring of those places. And each place has its own particular history, as Jennifer Robinson (2006) has argued in calling for an appreciation of each city as 'ordinary'. However, in order to make sense of migration processes and their variations, we need to theorize not only the agency of migrants, whose networks restructure a specific locality, but also the global flows of capital of various kinds, which contribute to stark differences between the competitive positioning of different localities with consequences for all the inhabitants of each city and town involved.

A global power perspective that addresses migration and its relationship to the neo-liberal restructuring of locality leads us to a more nuanced view of the impact of remittances than is currently available in the migration and development field. This global perspective highlights the dual role played by migrant remittances in relation to the impact of neo-liberal restructuring. On the one hand, the impact of the privatization of public services is somewhat deflected as migrant remittances pay for vital needs, such as health care, education, and infrastructure. On the other hand, remittance flows within a neo-liberal context highlight locational disparities that are no longer addressed by state policies that would aim to even out regional disparities. On the contrary, as the flow of wealth becomes concentrated in specific localities, and as these towns and cities reposition themselves within local and even global economies through this restructuring, states may further these disparities. For instance, they may facilitate air travel and other infrastructural developments and industries such as tourism in areas developed through

migrant remittances, while other places become back-
waters whose residents are severely disadvantaged. Yet
studies of development and migration tend to ignore both
the specificities of localities that migrants connect through
their networks of social relations and the insertion of
these locations within broader structural disparities of
wealth and power. It is important to assess how we frame
our questions and analyses and to identify which migrants
and which localities are winners or losers because of the
role played by migrants in restructuring processes.

The implications of this perspective are many for the
study of processes termed 'development' in sending countries and 'urban restructuring' in settlement countries.
Migrants are seen as remittance senders without sufficient
discussion of how migrants are positioned in a new locality in terms of class and occupation, why migrants should
want to send remittances, and to whom and where their
transnational relations extend. Migrants' cultural values
offer an insufficient explanation as to why migrants send
large amounts of remittances and frequently support family members living elsewhere. Such explanations cannot
address the fact that migrants from around the world—
with different concepts of family and moral obligation—
engage in very similar behavior when confronted by similar migration contexts.

The contexts that facilitate migrants sending remittances and investing in localities within their transnational field seem to be related to the conditions faced by
migrants in their place and country of settlement, as well
as those that confront relatives and other members of
their social network who have been 'left behind' or who
are living elsewhere. Because discussions of migration
and development have increasingly taken the sending of
remittances for granted, we have too little research on
this subject. However, existing ethnographies and surveys

about the remittance-sending contexts have indicated that remittances are sent under one or more of the following conditions: (1) when children, spouses, or parents are left behind; (2) when migrants face insecure conditions in a place of settlement because of racism, anti-immigrant sentiment, or other forms of political, social, or economic discrimination; (3) when migrants secure a steady income in their place of settlement, whatever its size or source; (4) when migrants suffer great status loss through the migration process and a remittance-receiving economy provides them with opportunities to maintain or improve their status and class position; and (5) when a possible remittance-receiving locality—whether a hometown or elsewhere—provides alternative economic possibilities, allowing the migrants to 'hedge their bets'. These factors taken together help explain whether or not a migrant establishes and maintains a transnational social field.

By linking migrants' remittance-sending patterns and motivations to the conditions that they experience in specific localities, we can better account for why some people remain committed to sending remittances or making investments transnationally, while others disengage. The restructuring of localities through neo-liberal processes described above may facilitate or diminish the ability of migrants to send remittances. For example, neo-liberal policies may lead to the increased hiring of part-time workers and the inability of migrants to find steady employment. Or the privatization of public services may mean that there is more demand for low-wage migrant labor and more possibilities for migrants to send money regularly to their hometown or homeland. And in the home locality, structural adjustment policies may lead to the reduction of transportation services and increased public insecurity, which would curb investments in businesses or new housing.

The Countervailing Hegemonic Processes Encapsulated in State Migration Policies and Development Discourses

Culture remains an important variable in a global power analysis of migration, but cultural differences between natives and migrants within a nation-state are not assumed to be the central topic of concern. Instead, a global power analysis queries not only points of contention in which migrants are constructed as culturally different but also the domains of commonality, social relations, openness, and conviviality between migrants and natives. Migration scholars often fail to address daily social activities that unite migrants and natives within workplaces, neighborhoods, and leisure activities. They also disregard the forces that construct differences, such as the intersections of the global-political economy and local forms of differentiating power, including those that racialize, feminize, and subordinate regions, populations, and localities. As a means of addressing these concerns, Ramón Grosfoguel (2008) argues for an analytical framework that he calls the "colonial power matrix." He is developing a scholarship that analyzes the role of repressive force and discursive power with regard to the North/South divide. Building on the work of Anibal Quijano (2000), Grosfoguel (2008: 2) speaks of the coloniality of power as "an entanglement or … intersectionality … of multiple and heterogeneous global hierarchies ('heterarchies') of sexual, political, epistemic, economic, spiritual, linguistic and racial forms of domination and exploitation … [T]he racial/ethnic hierarchy of the European/non-European divide transversally reconfigures all the other global power structures."

Grosfoguel (2008) emphasizes that the concepts of racial and gender differences and the hierarchies that they substantiate are central to the legitimization of the location and dominance of finance capital in Northern states and institutions. The coloniality of the power framework addresses the disparities of wealth and power that link together the lack of development in the global South, the root causes of migration flows, and the interests of migrants and financial institutions in investments in remittance flows. This framework brings together in a single analytical structure the processes of capital accumulation, nation-state building, the restructuring of place, and the categorization of labor by race and gender.

When applied to migration scholarship, the coloniality of power approach allows us to understand better the current contradictory forces that denigrate migrants while celebrating migrant remittances. We can assess how constructions of migrants are used to dehumanize certain sectors of the workforce in order to legitimate more readily their insertion in neo-liberal labor demands. The national discourses of exclusion—which portray migrants as unskilled, threatening, and disruptive invaders and which seem rampant in states around the world, from Singapore to Italy—contribute to the current neo-liberal labor regime. Dehumanized through rhetorics of national difference, migrant labor, which is increasingly contractual, meets the needs of localized neo-liberal restructuring more efficiently than the previous, and still current, situation of family reunion, asylum, and the use of undocumented workers as a form of flexible and politically silenced labor.

Over the last few decades, growing international competition led to the development of global assembly lines, with de-industrialized centers of capital in North America and Europe and the movement of factories to far-flung regions, where labor is cheap and unregulated. Tariff barriers were demolished, and untaxed export processing zones were established throughout the world. Today,

agricultural and industrial corporations based in Europe
and North America increasingly face a contradiction in
their production processes—the balance between near
and far production. This contradiction is heightened by
the huge rise in the price of oil and hence transport,
which means it is more profitable to locate production
processes closer to areas of high consumer demand. One
increasingly popular solution is to use a workforce that
is cheap and controllable. As many observers in Europe
have pointed out, these contradictions will be heightened
by the low birth rate and aging composition of European
and North American populations (Castles 2006).

For several decades, undocumented migrants—first in
the United States and increasingly in Europe—made up
the quiescent, hyper-exploited, and flexible workforces
needed within urban restructuring processes. They fur-
nished labor not only for agriculture but also for 'just-
in-time' production close to centers of capital and for
the various domestic and service industries needed in
restructured cities geared toward consumer industries and
tourism. In some countries in Europe, such as the United
Kingdom, asylum seekers and refugees have provided this
form of labor, both legally and illegally. The denigration
and criminalization of asylum seekers and the growing
capacity of bio-surveillance measures to limit mobility are
essential features of a transition to a form of labor more
fitted to the production needs of neo-liberal economies.

It seems likely that we are witnessing a movement
toward an EU labor regime made up of circulating labor
from within the European Union and new and very controlled forms of contract labor from elsewhere. As Steven
Vertovec (2007: 2) has pointed out: "Circular migration
is … being advocated as a potential solution (at least in
part) to a number of challenges surrounding contemporary migration." The expansion of the EU labor market by

the inclusion of accession states with labor policies that emphasize the merits of circulation are part of this larger policy shift. Contract workers and labor circulation are now hailed as arrangements that benefit all parties, and short-term labor contracts are increasingly part of the production process for agricultural and factory work in places as disparate as Canada and Albania.

Migration researchers are contributing to the legitimization of new forms of exploitation by emphasizing the benefits of transnational remittances while neglecting to address the severe and permanent restriction of rights that accompanies short-term contract work and the decreasing access of migrants to naturalization. Some migration scholars have continued to sing the praises of circular short-term migration with regard to development. For example, Alejandro Portes (2007: 272) has asserted: "Cyclical migrations work best for both sending and receiving societies. Returnees are much more likely to save and make productive investments at home; they leave families behind to which sizable remittances are sent. More important, temporary migrants do not compromise the future of the next generation by placing their children in danger of downward assimilation abroad."

This kind of rosy picture reinforces the desirability of the new migration regime of contract labor, which makes migrant settlement increasingly difficult. New migration laws leave migrants with only short-term options. Absent from this scenario of the benefits of circular migration are the increasing difficulties of sustaining any form of viable existence in many sending areas. Also absent are the dehumanizing aspects of short-term labor contracts with their dramatic restrictions on, or denial of, rights and privileges to the individuals who are producing wealth, paying taxes, and sustaining infrastructures and services to which they have no entitlement. The mantras about migrants as major agents of development are also part of this new global labor regime. International financial institutions have made migrant remittances a growing industry just at the moment when migrants may be less interested in transnational strategies and yet less able to choose to settle permanently in a new land.

Transnational migration has in part reflected a strategy on the part of migrants to avoid committing themselves since they were unsure of the long-term welcome they might receive in the states in which they were settling, even if citizenship rights were available and utilized. However, migrants sending remittances did make certain assumptions about the viability of local economies in the sending states. They assumed that there would be enough security of persons and enough of an opportunity structure for those with capital to support their own investment in a home and family. Increasingly, these assumptions no longer hold in many regions of the world due to environmental degradation, destabilization because of structural adjustment policies, and the hollowing out of national economies through trade agreements such as NAFTA and WTO restrictions. The result is continuing waves of migration as well as a possible growing disinterest among migrants to invest in their homelands. This may be linked to an increased desire to reunite families in the country of settlement and to unilateral rather than simultaneous incorporation. Transnational migration and connection are not inherent features of migration but rather reflect conditions in both localities.

By examining the relations between the neo-liberal restructuring of capital and the need for an ever more controllable and flexible workforce, the connections between the various and seemingly disparate trends in migration policy and discourse begin to emerge. Nationalist rhetoric and exclusionary policies pave the way for production regimes that rely on the capacity to control labor. The faceless migrating workforce is portrayed as potentially lawless border invaders who require restriction, regulation, and contractual constraints that limit their rights to change employers or challenge working conditions. The depersonalizaton of labor as contractual services allows for labor policy statements in which the separation of workers from home and family, without rights of settlement and family reunion, becomes good economic policy. The depersonalization of the process allows such workers to be categorized as unskilled, despite the fact that many of them have relatively high degrees of education and may be nurses, doctors, teachers, or university professors. Their willingness to migrate is integrally related to the structural adjustment and privatization policies in their home localities that reduced wages and ended state-funded public services that had provided employment for professionals.

At first glance, the 'global war for talent', in which multinational corporations compete for highly educated workers, would seem to stand outside the emerging labor regime that I am describing. However, short-term contracts with restructured rights of settlement are increasingly part of this labor market as well, although in many countries highly skilled professionals are still being allowed to settle. Such short-term contracts often regulate high-tech workers to ensure that the current workforce gives way to the next wave of newly educated and eager bodies and brains. Moreover, the very prominence and desirability of the sought-after few highlight the disposability of the faceless many, despite the fact that both labor streams are needed to sustain many contemporary cities.

The dehumanization of migrants allows for them to be manipulated and controlled as various forms of unfree contracted labor. Meanwhile, migrant professionals can be welcomed in specific places as contributors to the neo-liberal restructuring and rescaling of various cities. Also, migrant remittances can be relied on to transmit foreign currency to families, localities, and regimes left behind, enabling their inclusion, however unequally, in global patterns of consumption and desire. In short, these seemingly discrepant narratives are part of the globally structured and locally situated mutual reconstitution of social relationships and values that a global power perspective allows us to analyze. Such a perspective facilitates advocacy of alternative policies and agendas.

It is insufficient, however, to reduce the flood of anti-immigrant sentiments to a justification for exploitative labor. Returning to the coloniality of power framework and using it as part of our global perspective on migration can yield further insights into the current moment of anti-immigrant attacks and contradictory discourses. At the same time, this perspective highlights how US and European imperialist projects are simultaneously justified and obscured through a politics of fear that portrays migrants as the chief threat to national security.

I have noted that states are still important within the globe-spanning economic processes that mark our contemporary world, but of course not all states are equal. Unequal globalization rests on a framework of imperial states that serve as base areas for institutions that control capital, the productions of arms, and military power. These powerful states claim and obtain rights and privileges in states around the world and define the institutional limits of less powerful states. The core imperial states also are the key players in institutions that claim to be global, including the World Bank, the WTO, and the United Nations Security Council. Increasingly, theorists on the right and the left have recently returned to the concept of imperialism. They stress the significance of warfare, but often ignore the relationship between neo-liberal restructuring, migration, and the construction of images of the foreigner as enemy and terrorist (Cooper 2003; Ferguson 2004; Harvey 2003; Ikenberry 2002; Mann 2003; Reyna 2005).

In the face of intense global economic, political, social, and cultural interconnections and of growing inequality due to racialized and gendered hierarchies, the popularization of the notion of the migrant as the outsider rehabilitates earlier myths that nation-states contain homogeneous cultures shared by native populations. Once again, the migrant is constructed to reinforce and validate the nationalism that continues to socialize individuals to identify with their nation-state. Once again, a discourse that presents the world as divided into autonomous nation-states is becoming hegemonic.

Increasingly, as states are hollowed out in terms of infrastructure and discrete realms of economic production and are ever more integrally linked to production and consumption processes elsewhere, state narratives stress national identities and cultural difference. In short, nation-states are increasingly identity containers that maintain and disseminate images of the nation as a society that have little to do with the contemporary, transnational institutional structures within which social life and relations of power are produced. The less services and rights that states provide for their citizens and the more that they produce citizens who have been educated to identify as customers enmeshed in cultures of consumption rather than forms of civic and social engagement, the more that these states promote discourses of social cohesion and national community. The inside is increasingly constructed in relation to framing foreigners as the source of disruption—as being responsible for the decline of social services and of community. The more that ordinary citizens in states around the world find their futures circumscribed by poverty or lack of social mobility, the more that they are told by political leaders that the problems are caused by persons from elsewhere. Anti-immigrant discourse remains a nation-state building process, a ritual of renewal that engages its participants in defining their loyalty to a country by differentiating them from stigmatized and racialized others.

Conclusions

Migration studies too rarely address the global system that is reducing the opportunity for social and economic equality and justice around the world and the human costs of new short-term labor contracts. While potent critiques have been made about each strand of the contemporary and apparently contradictory narratives that address migration and development, the critiques remain encapsulated within different literatures. This has made it too easy to keep debates about migration separate from discussions of neo-liberal restructuring and the human toll that this agenda exacts around the world. Short-term labor contracts resurrect older forms of indenture, with limited rights and mobility. Families separated by migration regulations that allow no family reunion means the reproduction of social life at great personal sacrifice, with parents separated from children and spouses from each other, and elderly parents left to survive without the assistance of children. Developing a global power perspective on migration that directs attention to the contemporary neo-liberal moment allows us both to establish a research agenda that calls attention to the human costs of neo-liberal restructuring and to trace its various trajectories and the resistance it engenders.

A global perspective on migration can provide an analytical lens that would allow scholars of migration and development to think beyond the reimposition of nation-alist interests. Migration studies are at a crucial juncture. We can follow the pattern of the past, let our research be shaped by the public mood and the political moment, and revive old binaries, fears, and categories. Or we can engage in research that clarifies this moment by developing new frameworks for analysis. In short, we need a new scholarship that can build on our understanding of global processes and highlight them, so that we can actually document how migrants live their lives as constitutive actors in multiple social settings. This scholarship will reconstitute migration theory so that it explains current observations and facilitates new ones. To do this, we need to discard methodological nationalism so that our units of analysis do not obscure the presence of imperial globe-spanning power and its internal contradictions, its inability to provide consistent development, and its dependence on migrant labor.

The new scholarship should popularize the concept that migration and development processes are part of global forces experienced by people who move and those who do not move. This means that migration scholars must enter into the public debate about social cohesion by identifying the forces of globalization that are restructuring the lives of migrants and non-migrants alike and by speaking to the common struggle of most people of the world for social and economic justice and equality. When delimited by their methodological nationalism, migration theorists confine their units of analysis to the nation-state and the migrant. They are thus unable to track structures and processes of unequal capital flow that influence the experience of people who reside in particular localities. Migration scholars often fail to look at the relationships between migrants and natives that are not framed by concepts of cultural or ancestral difference.

Furthermore, they ignore the way in which local institutions that incorporate residents of states in a variety of ways are configured by power hierarchies that interpenetrate in states and regions.

Development discussions that laud migrant remittances yet do not address transnational fields of unequal power serve to obfuscate rather than promote analysis. Many states dominated by imperial power and its new regulatory architecture are struggling because a sizable proportion of their gross national product is channeled into debt service, leaving migrants to sustain the national economy through their contributions. Meanwhile, remittances and the flow of migrant capital across borders contribute to the profitability of banks and other financial institutions (Guarnizo 2003).

A global perspective on imperial power can also facilitate our ability as socially engaged scholars to theorize the contradictions of imperial dilemmas and find ways in which they can contribute to progressive social transformation. But we can do this only if we set aside born-again assimilationism and other forms of integrationist theory that posit migrants as disruptors of national communities. It is necessary for migrants and natives of countries around the world who find their lives diminished by unequal globalization to understand what the problem is and what it is not. It is not putative hordes of illegal aliens or migrants' transnational connections that are threatening the majority of people in the imperial core countries. Rather, we need to draw attention to the ways in which anti-immigrant rage and subjective feelings of despair, the precariousness of life, and life's unmet aspirations reflect and speak to the global fragility and exploitive character of contemporary capitalism, its restructuring of economies, labor regimes, and states, and its dependence on war and plunder.

Acknowledgments

Portions of this essay are built on a co-authored paper with Ayse Caglar entitled "Migrant Incorporation and City Scale: Theory in the Balance," which was delivered at the conference "MPI Workshop: Migration and City Scale," in Halle/Salle, Germany, in May 2005. Earlier versions of this essay were delivered at the Second International Colloquium on Migration and Development, "Migration, Transnationalism, and Social Transformation," in Cocoyoc, Mexico, on 26–28 October 2006; the Volkswagen Foundation Conference on Migration and Education, in Hamburg, Germany, on 22–23 February 2007; the RDI Conference on New Essentialisms, in Paris, France, on 22–25 May 2007; and the ZiF Conference on Transnational Migration and Development, in Bielefeld, Germany, on 30 May–1 June 2007. I wish to express my thanks to the conference organizers and participants, who are not responsible for the perspective of this essay. Special thanks are extended to the James H. Hayes and Claire Short Hayes Professorship of the Humanities, which I held; to Burt Feintuch, at the Center for the Humanities, University of New Hampshire, for summer support; to Günther Schlee, at the Max Planck Institute for Social Anthropology, for broader conceptualizations of integration and conflict; to Hartwig Schuck, for formatting and Web site posting; and to Darien Rozentals, for editorial assistance.

Notes

1. As Peter Kivisto (2005) has pointed out, the 'new assimilationists' are actually not that different from the old ones. Classic asssimilationists such Robert Park (1950) and Milton Gordon (1964) did not predict an inevitable melting away of cultural difference within the American crucible. In arguing their case for the new integration or when attacking immigrants for their

supposed failure to integrate, these scholars generally compare statistics on education level, workforce integration, and criminality that continue the divide between native and foreigner. They sometimes even compare different 'ethnic groups' without regard to questions of class background and national or local opportunity structures (Huntington 2000). For these integrationists, the defining and essential act continues to be the crossing of the border.

2. I have consistently been quoted as arguing that nation-states are declining in significance and as calling for a post-national world. I have in fact not taken this position. Together with most scholars of transnational migration, I view nation-states, with their legal systems, migration policies, and institutional structures, as significant for the establishment and persistence of transnational social fields (Basch, Glick Schiller, and Szanton Blanc 1994; Faist 2000; Glick Schiller 1999, 2003; Glick Schiller, Basch, and Blanc-Szanton 1992; Levitt 2001a, 2001b; Levitt and Glick Schiller 2004; Pries 2007; M. Smith and Guarnizo 1998; R. Smith 1998). Despite the now extensive literature on this topic, some analysts persist in accusing these scholars of ignoring the persisting importance of nation-states. See, for example, Bommes (2005) and Waldinger and Fitzgerald (2004).

3. The restrictions on the entry of persons from China beginning in 1882 constituted the precursor of US efforts at broader restrictive legislation. However, the gate was not shut against most migration until the 1920s. A law passed in 1917 not only continued the Chinese exclusion but forbade most Asian people from entering. Until 1965, the bulk of the restrictive legislation that followed was based on nationality. Migrants were categorized by country of origin, with tens of thousands of some nationalities being admitted, while no more than 100 of those of other national origins, including Greece, Bulgaria, Palestine, and Australia, were allowed. Most public discussions of the 1920s identified migrants by their nationality, popularizing the dividing line between Americans and those associated with other national origins.

4. In contrast to this general failure of transnational migration scholarship to theorize locality, Michael Peter Smith (2001) has developed a concept of 'transnational urbanism', which is intended to generate a new category of urbanism. The weakness of Smith's concept is that the category of transnational urbanism

readily becomes an ideal type, rather than an analytical tool through which to study specific localities and their various positionings as a result of regional history and global restructuring.

5. For important exceptions, see Dannecker (2007), de Haas (2007), Delgado Wise and Márquez Covarrubias (2007), Faist (2008), and Guarnizo (2007).

References

Alba, Richard, and Victor Nee. 2003. *Remaking the American Mainstream: Assimilation and Contemporary Immigration.* Cambridge, MA: Harvard University Press.

Barth, Fredrik. 1969. *Ethnic Groups and Boundaries: The Social Organization of Culture Difference.* Boston: Little Brown.

Basch, Linda, Nina Glick Schiller, and Cristina Szanton Blanc. 1994. *Nations Unbound: Transnational Projects, Postcolonial Predicaments, and Deterritorrialized Nation-States.* New York: Gordon and Breach.

Beck, Ulrich. 2000. "The Cosmopolitan Perspective: Sociology of the Second Age of Modernity." *British Journal of Sociology* 51, no. 1: 79–105.

Bodnar, John. 1985. *The Transplanted: A History of Immigrants in Urban America.* Bloomington: Indiana University Press.

Bommes, Michael. 2005. "Transnationalism or Assimilation?" http://www.jsse.org/2005/2005-1/transnationalism-assimilation-bommes.htm (accessed 30 December 2005).

Bommes, Michael, and Andrew Geddes. 2000. "Introduction: Immigration and the Welfare State." Pp. 1–12 in *Immigration and Welfare: Challenging the Borders of the Welfare State*, ed. Michael Bommes and Andrew Geddes. London: Routledge.

Brenner, Neil. 2001. "World City Theory, Globalization and the Comparative-Historical Method: Reflections on Janet Abu-Lughod's Interpretation of Contemporary Urban Restructuring." *Urban Affairs Review* 36, no. 6: 124–147.

_____. 2004. *New State Spaces: Urban Governance and the Rescaling of Statehood.* New York: Oxford University Press.

Brubaker, Rogers. 2004. *Ethnicity without Groups.* Cambridge, MA: Harvard University Press.

Caglar, Ayse. 1990. "Das Kultur-Konzept als Zwangsjacke: Studien zur Arbeitsmigration." *Zeitschrift für Türkei-Studien* 1: 93–105.

_____. 1997. "Hyphenated Identities and the Limits of 'Culture.'" Pp. 169–185 in *The Politics of Multiculturalism in the New Europe: Racism, Identity and Community*, ed. Tariq Modood and Pnina Werbner. London: Zed.

_____. 2005. "Mediascapes, Advertisement Industries: Turkish Immigrants in Europe and the European Union." *New German Critique* 92: 39–62.

_____. 2007. "Rescaling Cities, Cultural Diversity and Transnationalism: Migrants of Mardin and Essen." *Ethnic and Racial Studies* 30, no. 6: 1070–1095.

Castells, Manuel. 1996. *The Rise of Network Society*. Cambridge, MA: Blackwell.

Castles, Stephen. 2006. "Back to the Future? Can Europe Meet Its Labour Needs through Temporary Migration?" International Migration Institute, Oxford University Working Paper No. 1. http://www.imi.ox.ac.uk/pdfs/wp1-backtothefuture.pdf.

Cooper, Frederick. 2003. "Modernizing Colonialism and the Limits of Empire." *Items and Issues* 4, no. 4: 1–9.

Dannecker, Petra. 2007. "The Re-ordering of Political, Cultural and Social Spaces through Transnational Labour Migration." Paper presented at "Transnationalization and Development(s): Towards a North-South Perspective." Zentrum für interdisziplinäre Forschung, Bielefeld University, 31 May–1 June.

de Haas, Hein. 2007. "Migration and Development: A Theoretical Perspective." Paper presented at "Transnationalization and Development(s): Towards a North-South Perspective." Zentrum für interdisziplinäre Forschung, Bielefeld University, 31 May–1 June.

Delgado Wise, Raúl, and Humberto Márquez Covarrubias. 2007. "The Migration and Development Mantra in Mexico: Toward a New Analytical Approach." Paper presented at "Transnationalization and Development(s): Towards a North-South Perspective." Zentrum für interdisziplinäre Forschung, Bielefeld University, 31 May–1 June.

Esser, Hartmut. 2003. "Ist das Konzept der Assimilation überholt?" *Geographische Revue* 5 (Summer): 5–22.

_____. 2006. "Migration, Language and Integration." *AKI Research Review* 4. http://www.wzb.eu/zkd/aki/files/aki_research_review_4_summary.pdf.

Faist, Thomas. 2000. *The Volume and Dynamics of International Migration and Transnational Social Spaces.* Oxford: Oxford University Press.

_____. 2008. "Migrants as Transnational Development Agents: An Inquiry into the Newest Round of the Migration-Development Nexus." *Population, Space and Place* 14, no. 1: 21–42.

Fajnzylber, Pablo, and J. Humberto López. 2008. *Remittances and Development: Lessons from Latin America.* Washington, DC: World Bank. http://siteresources.worldbank.org/EXTLACOFFICEOFCE/Resources/RemittancesandDevelopment.pdf (accessed July 2009).

Fauser, Margit. 2007. "The Local Politics of Transnational Development Cooperation: On the Interaction between Migrant Organizations and Local Authorities in Spanish Cities." Paper presented at "Transnationalization and Development(s): Towards a North-South Perspective." Zentrum für interdisziplinäre Forschung, Bielefeld University, 31 May–1 June.

Ferguson, Niall. 2004. *Colossus: The Price of America's Empire.* New York: Penguin.

Gabaccia, Donna, and Fraser M. Ottanelli. 2001. *Italian Workers of the World: Labor Migration and the Formation of Multiethnic States.* Urbana: University of Illinois Press.

Gilroy, Paul. 1992. *The Black Atlantic: Modernity and Double Consciousness.* Cambridge, MA: Harvard University Press.

Glick Schiller, Nina. 1977. "Ethnic Groups Are Made Not Born." Pp. 23–35 in *Ethnic Encounters: Identities and Contexts*, ed. George Hicks and Philip Leis. North Scituate, MA: Duxbury Press.

_____. 1999. "Transmigrants and Nation-States: Something Old and Something New in the U.S. Immigrant Experience." Pp. 94–119 in *The Handbook of International Migration: The American Experience*, ed. Charles Hirshman, Philip Kasinitz, and Josh DeWind. New York: Russell Sage Foundation.

_____. 2003. "The Centrality of Ethnography in the Study of Transnational Migration: Seeing the Wetland Instead of the Swamp." Pp. 99–128 in *American Arrivals: Anthropology Engages the New Immigration*, ed. Nancy Foner. Santa Fe: School of American Research Press.

_____. 2006. "Introduction: What Can Transnational Studies Offer the Analysis of Localized Conflict and Protest?" *Focaal* 47 (Summer): 3–17.

Glick Schiller, Nina, Linda Basch, and Cristina Blanc-Szanton, eds. 1992. *Towards a Transnational Perspective on Migration: Race,*

Class, Ethnicity, and Nationalism Reconsidered. New York: New York Academy of Sciences.

Glick Schiller, Nina, and Ayse Caglar. 2009. "Towards a Comparative Theory of Locality in Migration Studies: Migrant Incorporation and City Scale." *Journal of Ethnic and Migration Studies* 35, no. 2: 177–202.

———, eds. 2010. *Locating Migration: Rescaling Cities and Migrants.* Ithaca, NY: Cornell University Press.

Glick Schiller, Nina, Ayse Caglar, and Thaddeus Guldbrandsen. 2006. "Beyond the Ethnic Lens: Locality, Globality, and Born-Again Incorporation." *American Ethnologist* 33, no. 4: 612–633.

Glick Schiller, Nina, Josh DeWind, Mare Lucie Brutus, Carolle Charles, Georges Fouron, and Luis Thomas. 1987. "All in the Same Boat? Unity and Diversity among Haitian Immigrants." Pp. 167–184 in *Caribbean Life in New York City,* ed. Constance R. Sutton and Elsa M. Chaney. Staten Island, NY: Center for Migration Studies.

Gonzalez, Nancie. 1988. *Sojourners of the Caribbean: Ethnogenesis and Ethnohistory of the Garifuna.* Urbana: University of Illinois Press.

Goode, Judith. 2010. "The Campaign for New Immigrants in Philadelphia: Imagining Possibilities and Confronting Realities." In Glick Schiller and Caglar 2010.

Gordon, Milton. 1964. *Assimilation in American Life: The Role of Race, Religion and National Origins.* New York: Oxford University Press.

Grosfoguel, Ramón. 2008. "Transmodernity, Border Thinking, and Global Coloniality: Decolonizing Political Economy and Postcolonial Studies." http://www.eurozine.com/articles/2008-07-04-grosfoguel-en.html (accessed March 2009).

Guarnizo, Luis. 2003. "The Economics of Transnational Living." *International Migration Review* 37, no. 3: 666–699.

———. 2007. "The Migration-Development Nexus and the Post–Cold War World Order." Paper presented at "Transnationalization and Development(s): Towards a North-South Perspective." Zentrum für interdisziplinäre Forschung, Bielefeld University, 31 May–1 June.

Guarnizo, Luis, Alejandro Portes, and William Haller. 2003. "Assimilation and Transnationalism: Determinants of Transnational Political Action among Contemporary Migrants." *American Journal of Sociology* 108: 1211–1248.

Hardt, Michael, and Antonio Negri. 2000. *Empire*. Cambridge, MA: Harvard University Press.

Harvey, David. 2003. *The New Imperialism*. Oxford: Oxford University Press.

_____. 2005. *A Brief History of Neoliberalism*. New York: Oxford University Press.

Heckmann, Friedrich. 2003. "From Ethnic Nation to Universalistic Immigrant Integration: Germany." Pp. 45–78 in *The Integration of Immigrants in European Societies: National Differences and Trends of Convergence*, ed. Friedrich Heckmann and Dominique Schnapper. Stuttgart: Lucius und Lucius.

Huntington, Samuel. 2000. *Reconsidering Immigration: Is Mexico a Special Case?* San Diego: Center for Immigration Studies. http://www.cis.org/articles/2000/back1100.html.

Ikenberry, John. 2002. "America's Imperial Ambition." *Foreign Affairs* 81, no. 5: 44–62.

Jessop, Bob. 2003. "The Crisis of the National Spatio-Temporal Fix and the Ecological Dominance of Globalizing Capitalism." Published by the Department of Sociology, Lancaster University. http://www.lancs.ac.uk/fass/sociology/papers/jessop-crisis-of-the-national-spatio-temporal-fix.pdf. (The paper was previously published at http://comp.lancs.ac.uk/sociology/soc043rj.html in 2000.)

Joppke, Christian, and Ewa Morawska. 2002. *Toward Assimilation and Citizenship: Immigrants in Liberal Nations.* Basingstoke, UK: Palgrave.

Kastoryano, Riva. 2002. *Negotiating Identities: States and Immigrants in France and Germany.* Princeton, NJ: Princeton University Press.

Kivisto, Peter. 2005. *Incorporating Diversity: Rethinking Assimilation in a Multicultural Age.* Boulder, CO: Paradigm Publishers.

Lapper, Richard. 2007a. "Building Futures." *Financial Times*, 29 August. http://www.ft.com/cms/s/0/1bf0b258-55d3-11dc-b971-0000779fd2ac.html (accessed 27 September 2007).

_____. 2007b. "The Tale of Globalisation's Exiles." *Financial Times*, 27 August. http://www.ft.com/cms/s/0/11c878de-54bf-11dc-890c-0000779fd2ac.html (accessed 15 September 2007).

Levitt, Peggy. 2001a. *The Transnational Villagers.* Berkeley: University of California Press.

_____. 2001b. "Transnational Migration: Taking Stock and Future Directions." *Global Networks* 1, no. 3: 195–216.

Levitt, Peggy, and Nina Glick Schiller. 2004. "Transnational Perspec-
    tives on Migration: Conceptualizing Simultaneity." *International
    Migration Review* 38, no. 145: 595–629.
Mann, Michael. 2003. *Incoherent Empire*. London: Verso.
Martins, Herminio. 1974. "Time and Theory in Sociology." Pp.
    248–294 in *Approaches to Sociology: An Introduction to Major
    Trends in British Sociology*, ed. John Rex. London: Routledge
    and Kegan Paul.
Massey, Douglas S., Joaquín Arango, Graeme Hugo, Ali Kouaouci,
    Adela Pellegrino, and J. Edward Taylor. 1998. *Worlds in Motion:
    Understanding International Migration at the End of the Millen-
    nium*. Oxford: Clarendon Press.
Mittleman, James, ed. 1996. *Globalization: Critical Reflections*. Lon-
    don: Lynne Reinner.
Morawska, Ewa. 2003. "Immigrant Transnationalism and Assimila-
    tion: A Variety of Combinations and the Analytic Strategy It
    Suggests." Pp. 133–176 in *Towards Assimilation and Citizenship:
    Immigrants in Liberal Nation-States*, ed. Christian Joppke and
    Ewa Morawska. London: Palgrave-McMillan.
Nye, Joseph S., Jr. 1976. "Independence and Interdependence."
    Foreign Policy 22 (Spring): 130–161.
Østergaard-Nielsen, Eva. 2007. "Perceptions and Practices of
    Co-development in Catalunya." Paper presented at "Trans-
    nationalization and Development(s): Towards a North-South
    Perspective." Zentrum für interdisziplinäre Forschung, Bielefeld
    University, 31 May–1 June.
Park, Robert E. 1950. *Race and Culture*. Glencoe, IL: Free Press.
Portes, Alejandro. 2007. "Migration, Development, and Segmented
    Assimilation: A Conceptual Review of the Evidence." *Annals
    of the American Academy of Political and Social Sciences Quick
    Read Synopsis* 610: 270–272. http://ann.sagepub.com/cgi/
    reprint/610/1/266.pdf.
Potts, Lydia. 1990. *The World Labour Market: A History of Migra-
    tion*. London: Zed Books.
Pries, Ludger. 2007. "Transnationalism: Trendy Catch-All or Specific
    Research Programme?" Paper presented at "Transnationaliza-
    tion and Development(s): Towards a North-South Perspective."
    Zentrum für interdisziplinäre Forschung, Bielefeld University, 31
    May–1 June.
Quijano, Anibal. 2000. "Coloniality of Power and Eurocentrism in
    Latin America." *International Sociology* 15, no. 2: 215–232.

Raghuram, Parvati. 2007. "Which Migration, What Development? Unsettling the Edifice of Migration and Development." Paper presented at "Transnationalization and Development(s): Towards a North-South Perspective." Zentrum für interdisziplinäre Forschung, Bielefeld University, 31 May–1 June.

Ratzel, Friedrich. 1882. *Anthropogeographie*. Stuttgart: J. Engelhorn.

Reyna, Stephen. 2005. "American Imperialism? The Current Runs Swiftly." *Focaal* 45 (Summer): 129–151.

Robinson, Jennifer. 2006. *Ordinary Cities: Between Modernity and Development*. New York: Routledge.

Salzbrunn, Monika. 2010. "Rescaling Processes in Two Cities: How Migrants are Incorporated in Urban Settings through Political and Cultural Events." In Glick Schiller and Caglar 2010.

Scott, Allen. 2004. "Cultural-Products Industries and Urban Economic Development." *Urban Affairs Review* 39, no. 4: 460–490.

Smith, Anthony. 1983. "Nationalism and Social Theory." *British Journal of Sociology* 34: 19–38.

Smith, Michael Peter. 2001. *Transnational Urbanism: Locating Globalization*. Malden, MA: Blackwell.

Smith, Michael Peter, and Luis Guarnizo, eds. 1998. *Transnationalism from Below*. New Brunswick, NJ: Transaction Publishers.

Smith, Neil. 1995. "Remaking Scale: Competition and Cooperation in Pre-National and Post-National Europe." Pp. 59–74 in *Competitive European Peripheries*, ed. Heikki Eskelinen and Folke Snickars. Berlin: Springer Verlag.

Smith, Robert C. 1998. "Transnational Localities: Community, Technology and the Politics of Membership within the Context of Mexico and U.S. Migration." Pp. 196–238 in M. Smith and Guarnizo 1998.

———. 2006. "Black Mexicans, Nerds and Cosmopolitans: Key Cases for Assimilation Theory." Paper presented at the Second International Colloquium on Migration and Development, "Migration, Transnationalism, and Social Transformation," Cocoyoc, Mexico, 26–28 October.

Sollors, Werner, ed. 1989. *The Invention of Ethnicity*. New York: Oxford University Press.

Swyngedouw, Erik. 1997. "Neither Global nor Local: 'Glocalization' and the Politics of Scale." Pp. 137–166 in *Spaces of Globalization*, ed. Kevin R. Cox. New York: Guilford Press.

Torpey, John. 2000. *The Invention of the Passport: Surveillance, Citizenship and the State*. Cambridge: Cambridge University Press.

Urry, John. 2000. "The Global Media and Cosmopolitanism." Paper presented at the Transnational America Conference, Bavarian American Academy, Munich, June. http://www.lancs.ac.uk/fass/sociology/papers/urry-global-media.pdf(accessed 20 September 2003).

van Holthoon, Frits, and Marcel van der Linden. 1988. *Internationalism in the Labour Movement, 1830–1940*. Leiden: E.J. Brill.

Vertovec, Steven. 2007. "Circular Migration: The Way Forward in Global Policy?" *Working Papers #4*, International Migration Institute Oxford University. http://www.imi.ox.ac.uk/pdfs/wp4-circular-migration-policy.pdf.

Waldinger, Roger, and David Fitzgerald. 2004. "Transnationalism in Question." *American Journal of Sociology* 109, no. 5: 1177–1195.

Wimmer, Andreas, and Nina Glick Schiller. 2002a. "Methodological Nationalism and Beyond: Nation-State Building, Migration and the Social Sciences." *Global Networks* 2, no. 4: 301–334.

———. 2002b. "Methodological Nationalism and the Study of Migration." *Archives of European Sociology* 43, no. 2: 217–240.

Wolf, Eric R. 1982. *Europe and the People without History*. Berkeley: University of California Press.

World Bank. 2006. *Global Economic Prospects: Economic Implications of Remittances and Migration*. Washington, DC: World Bank. http://www-wds.worldbank.org/servlet/WDSContentServer/WDSP/IB/2005/11/14/000112742_20051114174928/Rendered/PDF/343200GEP02006.pdf (accessed July 2009).

Zukin, Sharon. 1995. *The Cultures of Cities*. Oxford: Blackwell.

TRANSNATIONALIZATION AND DEVELOPMENT
Toward an Alternative Agenda

Thomas Faist

Public debate and research on the two-way relationship between migration and development—that is, on the migration-development nexus—have increased considerably over the past few years. To be more precise, interest in this topic has experienced yet another climax after two previous ones, in the 1960s and 1980s. However, there is very little systematic thought given to what is 'new' this time around. I argue that the current enthusiasm about the migration-development nexus should be approached from a transnational angle that recognizes the emergence of a new transnational agent in development discourse, variably called 'migrants', 'diaspora', or 'transnational community'. Increasingly, the cross-border ties of geographically mobile persons and collectives are being brought to the center of attention. National states, local governments, and inter- and supra-national organizations and development agencies seek to co-opt and establish ties with these agents, who are engaged in sustained and continuous cross-border relationships on a personal, collective, and organizational level. The emergence of this new type of development agent can be tackled by a decidedly transnational methodology, which allows us to look at what is usually called 'development' in both the North and the South. What this could mean in terms of concepts and research strategies is open for discussion. Instead of repeating the 'new mantra' (Ratha 2003) of migration and development, which is simply a rehash of previous debates in familiar terms, a useful starting point is to engage in two activities: first, to question the significance of the current debates, their economistic bias and their disjointed nature when it comes to North and South, and, second, to explore opportunities for a methodologically more sophisticated approach to trans-national linkages.

What Are the Elements of the New Enthusiasm?

The new enthusiasm around migration and development hinges on a number of strong claims, which in turn raise serious questions. These claims can be summarized in the statement that remittances (i.e., the flows of money, knowledge, and universal ideas) can have a positive effect on what is called development. Obviously, this is not a new insight. It has been part of familiar debates that have been on the public and academic agendas on and off since the 1960s. The first claim is that financial remit-tances carry a huge potential for poverty reduction and local investment, especially since remittances very often are resistant or even counter-cyclic to economic recession. The amount of remittances transferred to developing coun-tries through officially sanctioned channels, such as banks or money transfer services, is estimated to have increased sharply over the past several years—from about $40 bil-lion in 1990 to $167 billion in 2005 (IOM 2005: 270). This is at least double the sum of the annual Official Development Assistance (ODA) of the Organisation for Economic Co-operation and Development (OECD). Second, despite the fact that financial remittances still stand at its core, in this new round of enthusiasm—indeed, euphoria— more emphasis is placed on the transfer of human capital and social ideas and practices from the North to the South. With such shifts in ideas, the perception of costs and benefits has now changed, for instance, from 'brain drain' in the 1970s to 'brain gain' in the 1990s and 2000s. Nowadays, we supposedly find more win-win situations for mobile persons, states, and others. And even newer is the concept of 'social' remittances, the flow of ideas and practices that are 'good' and to which nobody in his or her right moral mind would object, such as human rights, gender equity, and democracy, to name only the most obvious ones. Third, part of the 'new mantra'—it has to be repeated a lot to be believed—is the desirability of temporary labor migration based on the expectation that temporary migrants will transmit a higher percentage of their income than permanent immigrants. This view was especially propounded by then UN Secretary-General Kofi Annan's Global Commission on International Migration in its 2005 report (GCIM 2005), which was given visibility by the United Nations High-Level Dialogue on International Migration and Development in 2006.

Overall, these three broad and promising claims are tied to migration control. It is the hope expressed by political institutions such as the European Union Commission (2005) that, in the long run, economic growth supported in part by financial, knowledge, and social remittances will reduce 'migration pressure' in the sending countries. Yet even a cursory glance at this new enthusiasm casts doubt on this optimistic agenda and raises three sets of obvious questions.

The first question addresses what is new and what is old about the new mantra on the migration-development nexus. Actually, after decades of research, there is a consensus regarding the consequences of migration on development, at least among economists: while the economic impacts for receiving countries, mostly OECD states, "have positive effects" (Delgado Wise and Covarrubias, this volume), the benefits for sending countries are less clear-cut and heavily contested. Most studies conclude that development in the countries of origin is not a result of migration and resultant remittances and investments by migrants. Rather, development—along with the right institutional conditions—is a prerequisite for migrants to invest and to remit meaningfully. These results have been evidenced over and over again. Therefore, there is a dire need to historicize the discourses on the migration-development nexus.

An examination of sustained cross-border transactions raises a second set of questions regarding transnational ties that are thought to be good—or bad—for development. Recently, terms such as 'diaspora' and 'transnational communities' are being used by scholars, politicians, and bureaucrats in both emigration and immigration regions. Also, some transnational transactions are being represented as negative in public discourse, such as references to fundamentalist Muslims, whose transnational religious ties lead them not to want to become 'like us', or to refugee or diaspora warriors, who want to establish new states by force. This is also the case for judgments about return migrants being made in regions such as Latin America and South Asia. For example, female return migrants who seek to acquire property and earn their own income may be perceived as threats to established patriarchal orders (Dannecker 2004). In short, the new enthusiasm overlooks the need for the renegotiation of boundaries and the political conflicts that are associated with transnational transactions, such as class-based, professional, ethnic, and gendered hierarchies. To counter this oversight, we need to take a closer look at the purposes for which a transnational perspective is being deployed and it potential outcomes.

Finally, it is important to ask why this new enthusiasm for migration and development has emerged at this particular point in time. How is it connected to changing paradigms in development thinking and the overall discursive embedding of concerns about migration into the trinity of the community/civil society, the market, and the state? How is it related to—or affected by—changing geo-political formations and forms of migration control following the demise of the Cold War?

What Is 'Old' and What Is 'New'? The History of Thinking on the Migration-Development Nexus

Taking a time frame of about 50 years, the fundamental claims associated with the current migration-development enthusiasm are not so new. From a simple cost-benefit point of view, the basic idea says that the flow of emigrants and the accompanying brain drain are partly or wholly compensated for by a reverse flow of money, ideas, and knowledge. It is interesting, yet not surprising, that the conceptualization of the nexus between migration and development mirrors the dominant development paradigms, with economics being the leading and most conspicuous discipline in conceptualizing development.

Of course, aspects of migration and phenomena that, after the late 1940s, have been called development figured much earlier than the 1960s. In their seminal work, *The Polish Peasant in Europe and America*, William Thomas and Florian Znaniecki ([1918–1921] 1927: 5:98–127) talk in detail about "the role of supra-territorial organizations." They begin their analysis with the attempts of Polish-American priests to bring together the representatives of the Polish colonies in America (*Polonia Americana*) and manage the common affairs of the American Poles. The authors then go on to discuss the role of Catholic, nationalist, socialist, and humanitarian organizations in structuring both adaptation in the United States and what later would be called modernization in Poland.

However, the term 'development' was not connected in explicit ways to migration in academic and public discourses until the 1960s. Starting at that time and continuing up to the present, the following three phases of the migration-development nexus can be distinguished.

Phase 1: Migration and Development—Remittances and Return

In phase 1, during the 1960s, public policy emphasized the 'labor gaps' in the North and 'development' in the South. The latter was supposed to result from financial remittances, return migration, and the subsequent transfer of human capital (Kindleberger 1967). This view clearly corresponded to overall economic modernization concepts and to a belief that state capacity could shape economic growth. Moreover, it was congruent with the economics textbook mantra, which suggests that the emigration of surplus labor from underdeveloped areas leads to a new equilibrium between capital and labor (see Lewis 1954). If labor goes North, labor scarcities in the South should then create an inflow of capital and, eventually, economic development in the South (cf. Hamilton and Whaley 1984).

Phase 2: Underdevelopment and Migration—Poverty and Brain Drain

In phase 2, during much of the 1970s and 1980s, the term 'development' came to be replaced by 'dependency' as a structural condition of the periphery dominated by a center, and 'underdevelopment' was seen as its inevitable result. During this period—in which dependency theory and then world systems theory à la Immanuel Wallerstein (1974) criticized modernization theory—the nexus was partly seen the other way around in terms of assumed causality, that is, not from migration to development but from underdevelopment to migration (see, e.g., Portes and Walton 1981). In terms of public policy, one of the central issues was not financial remittances, since most European countries had stopped recruitment and closed their main gates, keeping only side doors open for selected categories in the 1970s and 1980s. Rather, the key issue was that of brain drain. In a dependency perspective, underdevelopment led to the loss of highly skilled workers, who migrated from the periphery to the centers in the dependent world and, above all, into industrialized countries. This out-migration, in turn, was thought to contribute to even more underdevelopment and increased migration flows through asymmetric distribution of benefits and resources (cf. Martin 1991). Evidence for this thesis is easy to spot nowadays as well. For example, in 2005, between one-third and one-half of the so-called developing world's science and technology personnel lived in OECD countries (Khadria, this volume). And it is almost needless to say that a differentiated view of the movement of brains indeed has proven "brain strain hotspots" (Lowell, Findlay, and Stewart 2004), such as the health-care sector in sub-Saharan Africa, while countries developing quickly along economic lines, such as Taiwan, South Korea, and the

People's Republic of China, could change the situation into "reverse brain drain" (Zweig 2006).

Phase 3: Migration and Co-development—the Celebration of Circulation

In phase 3, which has been underway since the 1990s, the idea of what in French has been called *co-développement* best describes the public policy approaches of immigration countries to the migration-development nexus, at least those propagated by states such as France, the Netherlands, and the United Kingdom, as well as international organizations such as the World Bank. Originally, the term described local-level development activities, but it soon came to encompass a broader migration-development strategy. The term 'co-development' connotes a reversal of the nexus and has led us back to a more optimistic view, akin to the 1960s. International migration is supposed to fuel development in the South and East—the 'global South'—this time not only via financial remittances and human capital, but also via knowledge flows more generally and social remittances (Maimbo and Ratha 2005). There seems to be a current belief that more circulation of labor fosters more development by way of remittances, resulting in the recent policy recommendation of the Global Commission to increase opportunities for short-term labor migration (GCIM 2005).

As this short sketch suggests, different directions of causality within the migration-development nexus were emphasized in the three periods discussed. Interestingly, none of these discourses took note of the most obvious linkage, namely, the well-established economic relationship between development and migration. Processes of Western-style industrial-economic development are usually described as a means to decrease emigration. While there is evidence that this proposition may be true in the long run, economic development, as measured in conventional terms such as growth in GDP, is likely to produce even more migrants in the short- and mid-term (Faist 2000: 160–162).

What is New? Migrants as Transnational Agents—Transnational Methodology

While in phase 1, just mentioned, policy makers and analysts principally looked on remittances and return migration as a way of transferring resources across borders, in phase 3, the landscape of alternatives has widened in an era termed 'globalization', 'network society', or 'world society'—a period of ever-increasing circulation. All of the new terms, such as 'co-development', point to the emergence of new transnational agents, that is, 'diasporic' actors. Underlying this semantic change is the belief that migrants and geographically mobile persons, and those with whom they associate, may be engaged in sustained and continuous cross-border practices. So the story is not simply about migration and development, but also transnationalization.

Various agents have repositioned themselves locally due to global changes since the late 1980s. Both public policies and rhetoric have changed. A prominent example of the transformed political semantics involves the discursive and institutional changes that the People's Republic of China has implemented. Discursively, the slogan to 'serve the country' (*wei guo fuwu*) has replaced the previous motto, 'return to serve' (*huiguo fuwu*) (Cheng Xi in Nyíri 2001: 637). Such rhetoric has been complemented by public policy changes, including adaptations through mechanisms such as dual citizenship for emigrants and

immigrants (Faist 2007; Glick Schiller 2005), voting rights
for absentees, tax incentives for citizens abroad, and co-
optation of migrant organizations by local, regional, and
state governments for development cooperation. Instead
of permanent return migration, temporary returns, visits,
and other forms of transactions have moved to the center
of attention. Thus, in recent years the notion of migrants'
return as an asset to development has been complemented
by the idea that even if there is no eventual return, the
commitment of migrants living abroad could be tapped,
not only, for example, through hometown associations
but also through informal "diaspora knowledge networks"
(Barré et al. 2003). These networks include scientists and
R&D personnel, innovative business start-ups (cf. Rauch
2001), and professionals working for multinational companies (Kuznetsov 2006).

States, development agencies, and international organizations try to support the circulatory mobility of persons
so engaged, with the keyword being 'temporary return'.
Examples are UNESCO's Transfer of Knowledge through
Expatriate Nationals (TOKTEN) program or the Migration
for Development in Africa (MIDA) program of the International Organization for Migration (IOM), both of which
send migrants as experts back to their countries of origin
for short periods of time. Of course, governments also
try to tap into the activities of hometown associations,
although—seen in terms of financial remittances—they
represent only a small fraction of remittances within kinship groups. A prominent example is the Mexican federal
government's Tres-Por-Uno (3x1) program, in which
each 'migra-dollar' sent back by migrants living abroad
is complemented by three dollars from various governmental levels to go toward regional development projects.
More recently, Mexican banks have joined the fray and
announced 4x1 programs. The examples given suggest that

states and organizations have started to build programs on obligations and commitments felt by migrants toward home institutions. To use Albert Hirschman's (1970) terms, socio-political loyalty is used after geographical exit to exert economic pressure and sometimes political voice.

Much of the semantics focuses on community. Presently, the two most fashionable terms are 'diaspora' and 'transnational communities', but there is an interesting difference: 'diaspora' is used frequently in the development discourse, while 'transnational communities' appears in transnationalist literature. Both terminologies refer to "communities without propinquity" (Faist 2000). Such communities are built primarily not on geographical closeness but on a series of social and symbolic ties that connect ethnic, religious, and professional diasporas. However, the notions of diaspora and transnational community need to be unbundled and even rejected in order to get closer to a systematic analysis (Glick Schiller 2004, this volume). Rogers Brubaker (2005: 3) cogently observed that the "universalization of the diaspora, paradoxically, means the disappearance of the diaspora." In recent decades, there has been a telling change of meaning. First, in the 'classical' meaning, diaspora referred to forced migration and violent dispersal, whereas nowadays it denotes any kind of migration—hence the talk of labor, trade, business, and refugee diasporas (Cohen 1997). Second, in the classical sense, diaspora implied a return to an imagined or real homeland, whereas now it signifies simply some sort of sustained ties to the home country. In postmodern usage, this can even be lateral ties, that is, ties in which emigrants are connected not only to their immigration countries but also all over the globe. Third, in the old meaning, diaspora referred to various forms of diaspora segregation in the immigration country, whereas in the new meaning it designates a sort of culturally pluralist boundary maintenance in the host country (e.g., Gilroy 1993). While these are interesting shifts in meaning, the terms 'diaspora' and 'transnational community' are too restrictive in that they imagine a rather homogeneous cross-border social formation. They repeat the same mistake as much migration scholarship in assuming rather homogeneous national, ethnic, and religious groupings (Glick Schiller, this volume).

Transnational social formations and a systematic transnational approach present an alternative. Transnational formations—as well as fields and spaces—consist of combinations of ties and their contents, positions in networks and organizations, and networks of organizations that cut across the borders of at least two national states. In other words, the term refers to sustained and continuous pluri-local transactions that cross state borders. There are various ways to conceptualize transnational social formations, which can be looked on as part of more general societal configurations. Two prominent approaches are fields and spaces: the former refers to the inner logic of social action and can be extended to systemic approaches, while the latter concerns the spatial dimension of social life. A commonality is that they aim to overcome "methodological territorialism" (Scholte 2000: 56), that is, conflating society, state, and territory. They are also meant to overcome the conflation of society, state, and nation that results from "methodological nationalism" (Wimmer and Glick Schiller 2003).

The newest wave of the migration-development nexus raises several challenges to transnational approaches, and a discussion of three of them follows. As an overview, we can say, first, that migrant organizations, such as hometown associations, should be included (cf. Moja 2005), but we also need to look at the spaces in between associations, organizations, and communities. Second, we can see a disjuncture between development studies, on the one hand, and migrant incorporation studies, on the other, with the former emphasizing the South, and the latter being almost exclusively concerned with integration issues in the OCED-North. Third, while there has been some discussion on how remittances can alleviate poverty but also strengthen overall inequality in emigration regions, little attention has been devoted to the public policy mechanisms that could contribute to equality and social citizenship.

Methodological Rigor

Most empirical studies on transnationalization and development from a sociological or anthropological viewpoint focus on associations and organizations, a line of research that needs to be continued (e.g., Smith 2006). However, such studies should be complemented with those that analyze the spaces in between associations—transactions that criss-cross multiple associations, networks that form within associations, and engagements that are non-organized. Methodologically, the exhortation of transnational approaches to engage in multi-sited fieldwork and to follow the flow of persons, money, ideas, conflicts, biographies, and stories across borders (Marcus 1995) has not really been taken very seriously, contrary to most pronouncements. A more systematic network approach, not only in the metaphorical sense, is necessary, and there are models that show how to do it (Glick Schiller 2003). To take multi-sited fieldwork (i.e., simultaneous research in differing locations) seriously would require following financial or other transactions in tracing lateral connectivities to other immigration and emigration regions. A case at hand is the five-year study by Valentina Mazzucato (2007) in tracing transactions

involving persons, groups, and organizations of Ghanaian migrants in Amsterdam back to locations in Ghana
and in other regions of the world. Such a methodological approach does not presume concepts of world
society, which would presuppose too much unity and
systemic differentiation. In sum, exploring transnational
connectivities through multi-sited fieldwork enables us
to look at the great variety of societal forms. In particular, it allows us to trace the combination of a high
degree of local clustering with a relatively low average
path distance between nodes and hubs that are located
in different states.

Networks can be built around various categorical
distinctions, such as ethnicity, race, gender, schooling,
professional training, political affiliation, and sexual
preference. Ethnicity constitutes a particularly vexing
issue in transnational studies. On the one hand, a transnational approach should be able to overcome the ethnic
bias inherent in much migration scholarship. The fallacy
is to label migrants immediately by ethnic or national
categories. Scholars often presuppose that categories
such as Turks, Brazilians, and so forth matter a lot, since
they do in public discourse. On the other hand, methods
should be able to trace actually existing ethnic social
formations, such as networks of reciprocity, which are
of great importance, for example, in informal transfer
systems of financial remittances. This suggests that the
issue of the importance of ethnicity should be turned into
an empirical question.

Linkages between informal networks and formal organizations are also under-researched. Sometimes, for example, village associations celebrating cultural practices from
the homeland change function. In the case of the overseas
Chinese in Southeast Asia, there are 'old linkages' and
'new networks'. Village associations (*shetuan*) function as

an arena for businesspersons who are planning to invest in certain parts of China (Liu 1998). While overseas Chinese entrepreneurs' foremost considerations in deciding on investment in China are available economic opportunities and profitability, it is in village associations that ties based on place of origin, kinship, and dialect become useful as a foundation for establishing personal relationships (*guanxi*). Cultural affinities can facilitate effective personal and business relationships and thus play an important part in directing a substantial amount of investment and charitable money to the People's Republic of China (*qiaoxiang*, or native land).

Incorporation and Development

So far, incorporation and development studies are disjointed, even in transnational studies. Either studies take the perspective of the country or region in which immigrants live and, from a transnational angle, analyze issues of incorporation into labor markets, housing, education, and cultural pluralism, in addition to social security, state security, wage differentials, and so forth, or they deal with the effects of transnational ties on home countries, villages, and formations from which migrants originate— such as demographic dynamics, remittance flows, and cultural impacts—often involving an analysis of transnational flows. The former studies, preoccupied with effects on immigration regions, have entered into a dialogue with assimilation and multiculturalism perspectives, and the latter, focusing on emigration regions, with development studies. Yet the two areas are awkward partners. For example, studies have found that in the case of immigrants from Mexico, the Dominican Republic, and Colombia living in the United States, transnational immigrant organizations' members are older and better established and possess above-average levels of education (Portes, Escobar, and Radford 2007). Depending on one's conceptual predisposition, this could be interpreted to mean that transnationalism and assimilation are not opposites, or that a strong transnational orientation indicates a specific path of incorporation.

However, if not carried onward, such discussions miss the essence of a transnational approach, which is relevant not only for viewing incorporation in national terms. From an integrated North-South perspective, one has to look not only at remittances but also at potential 'reverse remittances', or two-way flows. There are clearly empirical findings of reverse remittances, which can be important especially at the beginning stages of the migration of persons or groups, for example, helping undocumented migrants to get papers and thus to legalize their stay. In a systems perspective, two-way flows also have to be seen from a long-term historical outlook covering several centuries. There was a co-constitution of what we presently call the North and the South: from early colonialism onwards, many resources flowed from the South to the North. These flows of information, knowledge, and economic resources were critical for regions such as Europe, the most obvious linkage being migration from colonies or former colonies to centers. In turn, such flows helped to create the very transnational remittance flows from the North to the South that we are looking at today.

It is questionable whether terms such as 'immigrant integration' or 'immigrant incorporation' are able to capture how two-way flows shape associational life in between emigration and immigration regions. They are valid perspectives, of course, centering on regions of destination and origin. These in-between transactions constitute social facts *sui generis*, but we have not yet found an appropriate terminology to deal with them. Simply reject-ing methodological nationalism is not enough.

Public Policy, Networks, and Inequality

Many studies look positively at remittances—financial, knowledge, and social—because they may reduce poverty or even eradicate it and contribute to economic growth. However, there is almost no discussion about the mecha-nisms by which this would come about—it is almost as if an 'invisible hand' would transform remittances into poverty reduction and economic growth. Needless to say, this is a very myopic view of the public policy rel-evance of remittances. If transnational migration is being linked to global social inequality, then remittances must be examined for their relevance to social policy. Seen in this way, they do not constitute explicit social policies, of course, but they form a basis for fostering social solidar-ity among citizens. This thought is not as far-fetched as it may seem at first. Comparative historians of welfare states tell us that 'late industrializers' (in the sense of Alexander Gershenkron), such as the Nordic countries and East Asia (Wong 2006), developed more universal social policies than 'early industrializers', such as the United Kingdom. Yet in the recent past, targeted social policies, in contrast to universal policies, were the foundation of approaches favored by international organizations in the case of developing countries. Such policies—in particular, Struc-tural Adjustment Programs (SAPs) and Poverty Reduction Strategy Papers (PRSP)—failed miserably.

Therefore, the crucial question is how to fit remittances into universal social policies. How can they be factored into what a recent publication by the United Nations Research Institute for Social Development (UNRISD 2007) calls "developmental welfare"? Social policy and social rights are not something that might simply evolve after a certain level of development has been reached; rather, "social policy is a key instrument for economic and social development" (ibid.: 2). Since there is no simple remittance-development nexus, we need to look at policies that can forge social solidarity and are thus based on social citizenship. All great theorists of societal membership—Aristotle, Cicero, J. S. Mill, Hannah Arendt, T. H. Marshall—have agreed that in order to participate fully in public life, persons need to be in a certain socio-economic and political position. In Marshall's ([1950] 1973) tradition we may call it 'social citizenship'; more recently, the term 'capabilities' has been introduced by Amartya Sen (1999) to capture the same thought.

In sum, there is, first, an interesting nexus between remittances, social policy, and development, with remittances constituting a sort of intervening variable because they are an expression of diffuse solidarity and generalized reciprocity upon which any kind of social policy has to be built. Second, only by integrating transnational migrants into policy circuits on various governance levels can such potentials be realized. Therefore, the uncritical celebration by both neo-liberal and transnationalist-cum-communitarian views of diasporas and transnational communities in isolation from other agents may be seriously misguided. At the very least, we need to analyze the social policy potential inherent in the transnational approach with respect to state agencies on various levels, non-governmental organizations, and economic organizations such as firms.

Why Now? Structural Factors Shaping the New Enthusiasm

The last broad issue I would like to touch upon in this essay is why the concepts of the migration-development nexus and migrants as transnational agents of development have been introduced at this time and how doing so fits into the changing paradigms and thinking on development. Three topics need to be considered: first, the discursive constitution of the relationships between the state versus civil society and community and the market versus civil society; second, geo-political changes since the end of the Cold War; and, third, migration control as an implicit factor driving circulatory migration.

Changing Concepts of Development: Statehood, the Market, and Transnational Civil Society and Community

The criticism of the 'civil religion' of development from the 1980s onward has called into question the idea of a homogeneous Third World, notions of progress (Rist 1996), and, most important for our inquiry, relations between the state and civil society and community (Schuurman 2000). The changing conceptualizations of the state, of civil society and the community, and of the market over the past 50 years in the development debate may signal a transnationalization of these terms. This can be usefully illustrated in the relationship between, first, the state and civil society and community and, second, the market and civil society and community. Crucially, development thinking has moved from a focus on the national state to more emphasis on local government and international institutions. Therefore, we have to broaden our concepts and speak not simply of 'the state' but of 'statehood' on various levels. Moreover, as the enthusiasm over the concepts of diasporas and transnational communities indicates, civil society also has to be conceptualized as a *transnational* civil society.

Statehood and Civil Society. While modernization theory promoted a strong belief in the crucial role of the

national state, this belief was called into question after
the 1960s and 1970s. At this time, international development organizations focused more on the market as a
principle, and diffuse notions such as community and
civil society became the lodestars of development. The
epitome of the market was the by now dated Washington
Consensus,[1] while community and civil society—often
used interchangeably—entered discussions in the context of strategies such as basic needs. It has been in this
context that migrants were introduced in the 1990s as
a civil society or community actor, either as individuals
remitting funds or as migrant associations in the form of
diasporic of transnational communities. It is therefore no
coincidence that organized groups, including hometown
associations in Mexico, returnee associations in Jamaica,
and charitable foundations in Egypt, have gained importance in discourse and policy making. In short, over the
decades, the central role of the national state has become
de-emphasized in favor not only of the market but also of
civil society and community.

Equally noteworthy is the now often made distinction
between the central and local state. In the face of decentralization and its attendant slogans, such as 'ownership'
and 'stakeholdership', local governments, along with civil
society and community, have assumed a greater role. The
migration-development nexus proved to be no exception.
In immigration states such as France vis-à-vis West African states, the aforementioned idea of co-development
in phase 3 of the migration-development nexus sees
migrants as their own development agents regarding
sending countries. Migrants and their diasporas alleviate poverty and help to solve conflicts, especially if local
governments work with diaspora groups to deliver better
results. Examples can be found in France and Spain. In
general, the focus on local governments and diasporas

has come to be especially relevant in cases where national states in Third World countries have failed to establish territorial domination and the rule of law, to institutionalize democracy, or to start sustained economic development. Hope is invested in the prospect of non-governmental organizations and local governments working in a synergetic collaboration with diasporas.

The Market and Transnational Civil Society. Not only have statehood-civil society relations changed but also the linkages between the market and civil society. Communities and civil society are becoming more and more a complement to liberal economic approaches in the era of the post–Washington Consensus. Two elements abound: liberal economic thought, on the one hand, and participatory approaches, on the other. Liberal economic thought would suggest that migrants are their own best development agents. A recent UK House of Commons report touting diasporas as development agents approvingly cites John Kenneth Galbraith (1979: 7), who described migration as "the oldest action against poverty."

The second element—that is, participatory and grassroots approaches—is usually to be found as well. The commitment of transnational migrants to their regions of origin is seen as compatible with the concept of the 'market citizen', who, by the way, is not necessarily a political citizen. Participatory approaches, as expressed, for example, by reports of the United Nations Development Programme (UNDP 2002: 1), focus on collective remittances. Not surprisingly, migrants' collectives in all forms—hometown associations, diaspora knowledge networks, businesspersons' networks, and even religious congregations—are now sought after by governments seeking, as usual, to establish their own interest groups.

Obviously, the study of transnational civil society is not
to be restricted to non-governmental organizations.

Geo-political Changes: The New Role of Diasporas

Migrants' opportunities to voice political viewpoints
concerning their homelands changed dramatically after
the end of the Cold War. In the 1960s, lobbying activities
of diasporas mainly took the form of protests against
the domestic policies of governments in the homelands
(Armstrong 1976). Cold War rivalries largely dictated
the effectiveness of these diasporic anti-government
campaigns (Shain and Barth 2003). Currently, although
national liberation diasporas (Kurds, Tamils, Palestin-
ians, and so forth) are still ongoing, their activities have
become more varied; for example, some diasporas have
portrayed themselves as carriers of democratization.
Even in the context of armed conflict and civil wars,
diasporas have assumed a more visible role. Violent
conflicts have caused some countries to collapse totally,
making them ungovernable; examples include Afghanistan and countries located in the Great Lakes Region of
Africa and the Horn of Africa. In these cases, the activities of immigration countries and development organizations have focused on conflict mediation in addition to
armed intervention (von Carlowitz 2004).

The Coupling of Migration Control and
Development Aid

Paradoxically, restrictive migration policies may be
conducive to financial remittances and transnational
kinship groups. Contemporary international borders are
much more akin to sieves than to medieval brick walls.
Their principal function is to protect the socio-economic,

demographic, and cultural integrity of the population that lies behind them. One important task is to filter out unacceptable or illegitimate migrants, while welcoming those who would increase the competitiveness of the economy. To paraphrase Ari Zolberg (1986), the hewers of wood and the drawers of water are implicitly 'wanted but not welcome'. By contrast, those migrants regarded as highly skilled, who transmit knowledge and foreign investments, are not only wanted but also quite welcome. The migration-development link is usually mentioned in regard to its function of reducing the propensity for migration to Europe. Coupled with such controls are policies making development aid to states in the European periphery conditional upon their willingness to restrict undocumented migration (Faist and Ette 2007). In other words, emigration countries need to show their willingness to control illegal migration to immigration countries in order to get development aid. One such country is Morocco, which partly depends on the European Union for financial contributions.

Yet these policies, provided that they are halfway effective, may produce unintended consequences. For example, the implicit migration policy logic of remittance and development discussions is that migrants should keep migrating in a rather restrictive migration control configuration, which sets migrants up to remit with family members being left behind. Restrictive immigration policy toward some categories of mobiles, especially illegal ones, produces ruptured transnational families, making remittances even more relevant. Seen from a functional point of view, the public policies that differ toward undocumented migrants and those who are highly skilled—restrictive in the former case and welcoming in the latter—are important for sustaining the same kind of effect, namely, the circulation of persons and other resources.

An Alternative Perspective

The nexus of migration and development is not well represented in globalization studies. Many of the often-cited works pay scant attention to the mobility of people (Albrow 2007; Castells 1996), and if they do, they often portray it in an affirmative way, depicting migrants as smooth interlocutors of cosmopolitan lifestyles (Beck 2007). With the exceptions of David Held and his collaborators in their sweeping account of global transformations (Held et al. 1999), there is an odd silence on mobility in general and on migration in particular, along with the concomitant societal changes. Yet there are glaring gaps, even in migration studies and development studies themselves. As a first example, migration scholars who subscribe to the migration-development mantra often have a naive notion of development, seeing it primarily on the level of the nation-state. They do not inquire about the recipients of the development or which notion of development is being considered. Most migration scholars now work almost exclusively on international migration, but internal migration is equally important, when we consider large-scale urbanization processes in Southeast and South Asia and other parts of the world. As a second example of gaps in these studies, development scholars, at least in the past, not only have neglected migration but have spoken as if there was no internal differentiation among migrants—despite the fact that there are glaring differences between migrants in their relationships to their countries of origin and destination, which could be voluntary or forced. Also obvious is the fact that development research has not considered mobility and migration as integral parts of the social processes under observation.

In general, it is high time to use elements of social theory to situate the current round of the migration-development nexus (Castles 2008). A social transformation perspective, inspired by classical works such as Karl Polanyi's ([1944] 1968) *The Great Transformation*, should be helpful in doing so. Polanyi's work on European transformations from the eighteenth to the twentieth centuries is no attempt at grand theory; rather, it includes a historical analysis of broad political and economic macro-processes, which ended up in the catastrophe of Nazism. It is not so much the particular political-economic focus that is inspiring but rather the viewpoint on broad changes. Social transformation refers to a fundamental shift in the way that societal life is organized. This shift goes beyond the continual processes of incremental social change that are always at work. It implies a kind of change in which all existing social patterns are questioned and many are reconfigured. Polanyi took the rise of market liberalism in the nineteenth century in all realms as his point of departure. Today, economic but also political and cultural globalization and new patterns of international political and military power are reshaping our world. In a reconsideration of the relationship among the processes of social transformation that accompany the present global reconstitution of capital and structures of power, migration, and development, I suggest that three crucial fields of social transformation can be highlighted: policy paradigms, organizations, and gendered orders.

Policy Paradigms

When talking about policy paradigms, an interesting question is why the new migration-development mantra has occurred at this particular point in time. There are several answers, which need further explorations. First, the World Bank is looking for new ways to fulfill its mandate,[2] and this is increasingly more difficult as new donors enter the market, such as China in Africa. Second, the development industry—among others, a child of the Cold War—is trying

to resuscitate itself following the end of the East-West
conflict. Moreover, the development cooperation complex
is always looking for new ways to connect the promise
of progress to agents who need to be included: peasants,
women, migrants, and so forth. Third, the migration-
development idea has an ideological appeal that crosses
several schisms. So-called neo-liberal proponents of the
(former) Washington Consensus, whose hopes are vested
in individual remittances and investments, can support
with it, as can grassroots advocates who propagate collective action and are thus fond of collective remittances.
Fourth, the framework in which development is supposed
to proceed has changed significantly. Gone are the days
of the development state, which is now to be replaced by
'good governance' as epitomized by the rule of law and
democratization, in which there is ample room not only for
the local state but also for civil society actors and public-
private partnerships. Migrants and migrant associations fit
right into the growing importance of civil society agents.

   Along with changing state-civil society interactions,
state-citizen relations have also been undergoing change.
Emigration country governments have taken a renewed
interest in emigrants abroad, who increasingly self-
describe themselves as diasporic. To use Hirschman's
(1970) terms, international migration is a way to connect
both exit and voice, provided that those who have left
engage in political transactions across borders. What is
currently decisive is that governments and other interested agents such as development organizations tap into
the loyalty of international migrants. How is this possible,
since exit is a sign of weak loyalty to the state in the first
place? One of the answers can be grasped when looking at
the institution of citizenship. Emigrants who leave a state
do not automatically lose their full membership in their
homeland. The expansion of migrants' citizenship rights

can be motivated by the goal of increasing migrants' sense of commitment and contributions to the development of the emigration country. Under circumstances of increasing remittances, some governments change their rhetoric: migrants are no longer portrayed as 'traitors' but rather as 'national heroes'. What can be ascertained with confidence is that some of the most significant measures to maintain migrants' links with their country of origin have been those that enable them to engage in the domestic political process, for example, dual citizenship and external voting rights (Faist and Kivisto 2008), in addition to devices such as tax incentives.

Organizations

Migrant associations are currently constituted, and constitute themselves, as development agents (de Haas 2006), and it is worthwhile taking a closer look at what they actually do. Empirical evidence of migrant associations related to sending countries such as India, Turkey, the Philippines, Mexico, and Morocco suggests that many of them do not simply run development projects. They are also important in regard to transnationalism and for creating an environment in which the effects of social transformation are cushioned or can more easily be dealt with (Castles and Delgado Wise 2008). The emphasis of their work is on supporting migrants by improving their quality of life, often through better access to rights and political voice in both immigration and emigration regions. Thus, their activities may be relevant in terms of conditions for investment, legal and political reform, and so forth.

Several questions arise in this context. First, is the responsibility for development increasingly being placed upon the agency of migrants rather than on institutional structures? While it is clear that international migrants can influence these structures, they are minorities in virtually any population. In addition, this situation is aggravated by the fact that there are many more internal than international migrants. Second, and more fundamentally, in glorifying migrant associations as the harbinger of a sort of 'migrant civil society', is there a danger in reifying migration as something separate from development—in highlighting it as a 'thing apart' that can be used to promote development? And, third, what is the role of migrant associations, for example, hometown associations? It is true that there is spillover from sending to receiving countries and backwards, and that there are great potentials and empirically observable effects, at least locally. However, the content and form of this spillover involving migrant organizations are not determined in advance. The transnational ties that link home and host countries and other regions also provide the means and causes for conflict to occur among migrants, between migrants and relatively immobile stay-at-homes, and between migrant associations and states both local and otherwise. In sum, it is necessary to open up the 'black box' of internal associational politics.

Gendered Orders

Gender order is an important field for gauging the constitution of agents on various levels, both discursively and structurally. Discursively, one can easily see how migrants are portrayed in very contradictory ways, whether as national heroes, who contribute to national development, or as (global) victims, whose rights are violated. Structurally, we need to go beyond a sort of one-category analysis. In many publications we can read of the 'feminization' of international migration. What this means is that presently a higher percentage of migrants is made up of women than has previously been the case, although there have always been movements of women, on their own, over hundreds of years. But what is the significance of this current trend with regard to the migration-development nexus and the analysis of the mantra? In the mantra, women appear as bearers of social remittances and are portrayed in some accounts as being even more reliable remitters than men. They are also seen as transporting ideas about gender equity. Likewise, we could imagine accounts of men as bearers of social remittances who favor patriarchy. Is this the case empirically?

Gendered orders are never only about gender but are cross-cut by several other distinctions that are relevant for a discussion of inequality and development. This is the case even if we focus on gender and not only race/ethnicity and class (as in the famous triad, race, class, and gender) but also age, legal status, and health conditions. The criteria of membership, such as country of origin, religion, or gender, are defined by migrants depending on the situation, the contact person, and the context. The basic point, then, is to look at the circumstances in which distinctions, such as the gender distinction, assume relevance and what their cross-cutting inferences are. One of the ways to think about the inferences is the concept of intersectionality, that is, the relationship between multiple dimensions of social relations and social identities (Collins 1990). For example, it would be hard to understand the position of migrant men and women in certain sectors if we focused only on gendered positions. If we looked at only one category—gender—we would then see how men and women are slotted in specific job categories and niches, such as migrant women from the Philippines in care or household work and men in construction jobs. But we need to go beyond this relationship if we want to account for the effect that it has on gendered orders: we need to ask about social class. For example, we may arrive at the result that migrant women in care work may reinforce gendered classifications and stereotypes in labor markets in receiving countries, enabling men and women to engage in careers. Moreover, gendered orders differ along categories such as social class among migrants themselves. For example, migrant women in care work face very different opportunities and constraints compared to those who are classified as highly skilled IT workers. Similar considerations apply to men.

Conclusion: Continuous Social Change and Social Transformation

As I have demonstrated, the migration-development man-tra and research on the migration-development nexus display obvious elements of continuity. Presently, as in the 1960s and 1970s, migrants are described as indi-viduals and as collectives (e.g., diasporas, hometown associations), which fulfills the brokerage functions. As mentioned earlier, return migrants were previously seen as transferring the right kind of work ethics from immigra-tion to emigration countries, whereas nowadays they are the brokers of ideas about gender equity and initiators of processes of democratization. It seems as if this signals the recycling of modernization assumptions that have been prevalent since the 1950s and have constituted the core of development as progress around the world. Nonethe-less, we can also observe elements that could herald more far-reaching social transformations, although the trends are somewhat ambiguous and sometimes contradictory. One example involves diasporas. During the Cold War, emigrant associations tried to work their way into the web of East-West confrontations between the superpowers in the Third World. Theirs was a role of drawing boundar-ies globally along ideological lines. These days, diasporas have reinvented themselves as development agents and sometimes even receive funding from development agencies, both state and non-state. Yet this role is insufficiently captured if we look at only the development aspect. Any analysis has to take into account a broader frame of the transformation of states and capital, along with notions such as the "competition state" (Cerny 1997). As an example, the European Commission has discussed new migration schemes as necessary because of the competition of the European Union with the United States over highly skilled labor. Here, the frame of reference is competition between economic blocs. Looking at official documents, it becomes quite clear that development aspects, such as 'mobility partnership' with African countries, are tagged onto an ambitious agenda of attracting the 'best and brightest' talent from around the world.

In addition to competition, the endogenous logic of EU expansion implies traces of imperial statehood. The expansion of the European Union into Eastern Europe, for example, has been accompanied by bringing in bordering states as buffer zones for migration control and by seeking cooperation to ensure 'migration management'. In the case of North and West African countries, it has been even more difficult to secure this cooperation because there is no prospect of joining the European Union any time soon. Nonetheless, adding development cooperation to the control of international migration can be a powerful idea. For example, all of the treaties and accords that the European Union concludes with third countries contain a passage on migration and development. These migration control partnerships between the EU and transit countries have consequences that go beyond migrations to the European Union and that affect the mobility of migrants within, for example, Africa. African states have increasingly institutionalized migration controls in separate departments and ministries. In sum, the further advance of the competition state and the expansion of the European Union signal far-reaching changes of a socially transformative kind.

Finally, it is unlikely that the migration-development mantra will be sustained at its present level in the policy debates and in research. After all, it tends to elevate the comparatively small number of international migrants into an unwarranted instrumental role in development and diverts attention from much more prominent obstacles to development. Nevertheless, this trend may result in the constitution of yet another civil society actor in the realm of deeply asymmetric development cooperation. Governments, international organizations, and diaspora associations may well begin to form alliances to further their specific causes.

Although methodological considerations are not a special field, such as policy or research paradigms, organizational change, or the transformation of gendered orders, they are crucial. A critique of methodological nationalism is pivotal because a transnational lens—with the 'trans' emphasizing a transformative and not simply a transnational charac-ter—aims to overcome unhelpful binaries, such as refugee versus labor migrant, or sending versus receiving state. The transnational approach does not necessitate a whole that subsumes its parts, or systems that delineate lower orders such as organizations and interactions. Currently, there is a pressing need to draw the contours of methodological transnationalism. What is certain is that the critique of methodological nationalism would go completely wrong if it insisted on the declining importance of the national state in social transformation. On the contrary, looking at the nation-state through a transnational lens helps us to under-stand the important role of institutional agents such as states in an ever-denser web of power politics that involves international organizations, multinational companies, and NGOs (Levitt and Glick Schiller 2004).

Notes

1. The term 'Washington Consensus' was initially coined in 1989 by economist John Williamson to describe a set of 10 specific economic policy prescriptions (e.g., fiscal policy discipline, redirection of public spending, trade liberalization) that he considered should constitute the 'standard' reform package promoted for crisis-wracked developing countries by institutions such as the International Monetary Fund (IMF), the World Bank, and the US Treasury Department. Subsequently, the term has come to be used in a different and broader sense, as a synonym for market fundamentalism. In this way, the term has been associated with neo-liberal policies in general and has entered the wider debate over the expanding role of the free market and constraints upon state social and economic policies.
2. The mandate of the World Bank is to provide loans and credits to developing countries for projects that alleviate poverty and provide social and economic development.

References

Albrow, Martin. 2007. *Das globale Zeitalter*. Frankfurt am Main: Suhrkamp.

Armstrong, James A. 1976. "Mobilized and Proletarian Diasporas." *American Political Science Review* 70, no. 2: 393–408.

Barré, Philippe, Victor Hernandez, Jean-Baptiste Meyer, and Dominique Vinck, eds. 2003. *Diasporas scientifiques: Comment les pays en développement peuvent-ils tirer parti de leurs chercheurs et de leurs ingénieurs?* Paris: IRD Editions.

Beck, Ulrich. 2007. *Weltrisikogesellschaft*. Frankfurt am Main: Suhrkamp.

Brubaker, Rogers. 2005. "The 'Diaspora' Diaspora." *Ethnic and Racial Studies* 28, no. 1: 1–19.

Castells, Manuel. 1996. *The Rise of Network Society*. Oxford: Blackwell.

Castles, Stephen. 2008. "Development and Migration—Migration and Development: What Comes first?" Paper presented at the Social Science Research Council Conference, New York City, 28 February–1 March 2008. http://www.imi.ox.ac.uk/pdfs/

S%20Castles%20Mig%20and%20Dev%20for%20SSRC%20
April%2008.pdf (accessed 12 October 2009).

Castles, Stephen, and Raúl Delgado Wise, eds. 2008. *Migration and Development: Perspectives from the South*. Geneva: International Organization for Migration (IOM).

Cerny, Philip G. 1997. "Paradoxes of the Competition State: The Dynamics of Political Globalisation." *Government and Opposition* 32, no. 2: 251–274.

Cohen, Robin. 1997. *Global Diasporas: An Introduction*. London: University College London Press.

Collins, Patricia Hill. 1990. *Black Feminist Thought: Knowledge, Consciousness, and Empowerment*. Boston: Unwin Hyman.

Dannecker, Petra. 2004. "Transnational Migration and the Transformation of Gender Relations: The Case of Bangladeshi Labor Migrants." *Current Sociology* 53, no. 4: 655–674.

de Haas, Hein. 2006. *Engaging Diasporas: How Governments and Development Agencies Can Support Diaspora Involvement in the Development of Origin Countries*. Oxford: International Migration Institute, University of Oxford.

European Union Commission. 2005. *Migration and Development: Some Concrete Orientations*. Brussels: Commission of the European Communities. http://eur-lex.europa.eu/LexUriServ/LexUriServ.do?uri=COM:2005:0390:FIN:EN:PDF.

Faist, Thomas. 2000. *The Volume and Dynamics of International Migration and Transnational Social Spaces*. Oxford: Oxford University Press.

———, ed. 2007. *Dual Citizenship in Europe: From Nationhood to Societal Integration*. Avebury: Ashgate.

Faist, Thomas, and Andreas Ette, eds. 2007. *The Europeanization of National Policies and Politics of Immigration: Between Autonomy and the European Union*. Houndmills: Palgrave Macmillan.

Faist, Thomas, and Peter Kivisto, eds. 2008. *Dual Citizenship in Global Perspective: From Unitary to Multiple Citizenship*. Houndmills: Palgrave Macmillan.

Galbraith, John Kenneth. 1979. *The Nature of Mass Poverty*. Cambridge, MA: Harvard University Press.

GCIM (Global Commission on International Migration). 2005. *Migration in an Interconnected World: New Directions for Action*. Geneva: Global Commission on International Migration.

Gilroy, Paul. 1993. *The Black Atlantic: Modernity and Double Consciousness*. London: Verso.

Glick Schiller, Nina. 2003. "The Centrality of Ethnography in the Study of Transnational Migration: Seeing the Wetland Instead of the Swamp." Pp. 99–128 in *American Arrivals*, ed. Nancy Foner. Santa Fe, NM: School of American Research.

———. 2004. "Transnationality." Pp. 44–67 in *A Companion to the Anthropology of Politics*, ed. David Nugent and Joan Vincent. Malden, MA: Blackwell.

———. 2005. "Long Distance Nationalism." Pp. 70–80 in *Encyclopedia of Diasporas: Immigrant and Refugee Cultures Around the World, Vol. 1*, ed. Melvin Ember, Carol R. Ember, and Ian Skoggard. New York: Kluwer Academic/Plenum Publishers.

Hamilton, Bob, and John Whaley. 1984. "Efficiency and Distributional Implications of Global Restrictions on Labor Mobility." *Journal of Development Economics* 14, no. 1: 61–75.

Held, David, Anthony McGrew, David Goldblatt, and Jonathan Perraton. 1999. *Global Transformations: Politics, Economics and Culture*. Stanford, CA: Stanford University Press.

Hirschman, Albert. 1970. *Exit, Voice, and Loyalty*. Cambridge, MA: Harvard University Press.

IOM (International Organization for Migration). 2005. *World Migration: Costs and Benefits of International Migration*. Geneva: IOM.

Kindleberger, Charles P. 1967. *Europe's Postwar Growth: The Role of Labor Supply*. Cambridge, MA: Harvard University Press.

Kuznetsov, Yevgeny, ed. 2006. *Diaspora Networks and the International Migration of Skills: How Countries Can Draw on Their Talent Abroad*. Washington, DC: World Bank.

Levitt, Peggy, and Nina Glick Schiller. 2004. "Conceptualizing Simultaneity: A Transnational Social Field Perspective on Society." *International Migration Review* 38, no. 3: 1002–1040.

Lewis, Arthur W. 1954. *Theory of Economic Growth*. London: Unwin.

Liu, Hong. 1998. "Old Linkages, New Networks: The Globalization of Overseas Chinese Voluntary Associations and Its Implications." *China Quarterly* 155: 582–609.

Lowell, Lindsay B., Allan Findlay, and Emma Stewart. 2004. "Brain Strain: Optimising Highly Skilled Migration from Developing Countries." Asylum and Migration Working Paper No. 3, Institute for Public Policy Research, London.

Maimbo, Samuel Munzele, and Dilip Ratha, eds. 2005. *Remittances: Development Impact and Future Prospects*. Washington, DC: World Bank.

Marcus, George E. 1995. "Ethnography in/of the World System: The Emergence of Multi-Sited Ethnography." *Annual Review of Anthropology* 24: 95–117.

Marshall, T. H. [1950] 1973. *Citizenship and Social Class*. Cambridge: Cambridge University Press.

Martin, Philip L. 1991. *The Unfinished Story: Turkish Labor Migration in Western Europe, with Special Reference to the Federal Republic of Germany*. Geneva: International Labour Organization (ILO).

Mazzucato, Valentina. 2007. "The Role of Transnational Networks and Legal Status in Securing a Living: Ghanaian Migrants in the Netherlands." Working Paper No. 43, ESRC Centre on Migration, Policy and Society, University of Oxford.

Moja, Jose C. 2005. "Immigrants and Associations: A Global and Historical Perspective." *Journal of Ethnic and Migration Studies* 31, no. 5: 833–864.

Nyíri, Pál. 2001. "Expatriating Is Patriotic? The Discourse on 'New Migrants' in the People's Republic of China and Identity Construction among Recent Migrants from the PRC." *Journal of Ethnic and Migration Studies* 27, no. 4: 635–654.

Polanyi, Karl. [1944] 1968. *The Great Transformation: The Political and Economic Origins of Our Time*. 9th printing. Boston: Beacon Press.

Portes, Alejandro, Cristina Escobar, and Alexandria Walton Radford. 2007. "Immigrant Transnational Organizations and Development: A Comparative Study." *International Migration Review* 41, no. 1: 242–281.

Portes, Alejandro, and John Walton. 1981. *Labor, Class, and the International System*. New York: Academic Press.

Ratha, Dilip. 2003. "Workers' Remittances: An Important and Stable Source of External Development Finance." *Global Development Finance 2003*. Washington, DC: World Bank.

Rauch, James E. 2001. "Business and Social Networks in International Trade." *Journal of Economic Literature* 34: 1177–1204.

Rist, Gilbert. 1996. *Le développement: Histoire d'une croyance occidentale*. Paris: Presses de Sciences Po.

Scholte, Jan Aart. 2000. *Globalization: A Critical Introduction*. Basingstoke: Macmillan.

Schuurman, Frans J. 2000. "Paradigms Lost, Paradigms Regained? Development Studies in the Twenty-First Century." *Third World Quarterly* 21, no. 1: 7–20.

Sen, Amartya K. 1999. *Development as Freedom*. New York: Knopf.

Shain, Yossi, and Aharon Barth. 2003. "Diasporas and International Relations Theory." *International Organization* 57, no. 3: 449–479.

Smith, Robert C. 2006. *Mexican New York: Transnational Lives of New Immigrants.* Berkeley: University of California Press.

Thomas, William I., and Florian Znaniecki. [1918–1921] 1927. *The Polish Peasant in Europe and America.* 5 vols. New York: Alfred A. Knopf.

UNDP (United Nations Development Programme). 2002. *Human Development Report 2001: Making New Technologies Work for Human Development.* New York: UNDP.

UNRISD (United Nations Research Institute for Social Development). 2007. "Transformative Social Policy: Lessons from UNRISD Research." Research and Policy Briefs, No. 5. http://www.unrisd.org/UNRISD/website/document.nsf/ab82a6805797760f80256b4f005da1ab/c77a2891bc2fd07fc12572130020b2ac/$FILE/RPB5e.pdf (accessed 28 May 2007).

von Carlowitz, Leopold. 2004. "Migranten als Garanten? Über die Schwierigkeiten beim Rechtsstaatsexport in Nachkriegsgesellschaften." HSFK Standpunkte No. 6. Frankfurt am Main: Hessische Stiftung für Friedens- und Konfliktforschung.

Wallerstein, Immanuel. 1974. *The Modern World System: Capitalist Agriculture and the Origins of the European World-Economy in the Sixteenth Century.* New York: Academic Press.

Wimmer, Andreas, and Nina Glick Schiller. 2003. "Methodological Nationalism, the Social Sciences, and the Study of Migration: An Essay in Historical Epistemology." *International Migration Review* 37, no. 4: 576–610.

Wong, Joseph. 2006. *Healthy Democracies: Welfare Politics in Taiwan and South Korea.* Ithaca, NY: Cornell University Press.

Zolberg, Aristide R. 1986. "'Wanted But Not Welcome': Alien Labor in Western Development." Pp. 36–73 in *Population in an Interacting World,* ed. William Alonso. Cambridge, MA: Harvard University Press.

Zweig, David. 2006. "Learning to Compete: China's Efforts to Encourage a 'Reverse Brain Drain.'" Pp. 187–215 in *Competing for Global Talent,* ed. Christiane Kuptsch and Pang Eng Fong. Geneva: International Labour Organization (ILO).

POLITICIZING THE TRANSNATIONAL

On Implications for Migrants, Refugees, and Scholarship

Riina Isotalo

Development, politics, migration, and refugeeness are integrally linked. Economic disparities between developing and developed countries have long been seen as key determinants of migration (Sørensen 2004). However, assessments of the impact of migration on the dynamics of development have varied over time and have not been conducted systematically (ibid.). My viewpoint is that, within transnational studies, security-related disparities between developing and developed countries that serve as determinants of migration have been studied even less systematically.

This essay is concerned with the development and security policy implications of transnationality. However, I am not addressing this topic from within development, by way of looking at how migrants' transnational practices can be utilized to further development. Several analysts have explored that area (see, e.g., Levitt and Sørensen 2004, as well as the essays in this volume)[1] and, while doing so, have identified wide gaps in research. Moreover, my interest in transnationality extends beyond the topics of transnational politics and political transnationalism (Østergaard-Nielsen 2003; Piper 2006), which address long-distance nationalism, migrants' engagement in homeland politics, and a diaspora's role in resolving or perpetuating conflicts. Instead, I approach the development-politics-migration-refugeeness nexus through an examination of the multi-dimensional phenomenon that I refer to as the 'politicization of the transnational paradigm'.

The number of people on the move has risen considerably during the last three decades. Today, the estimated number of international migrants is approximately 190,600,000,[2] but the de facto figures are probably much higher. Accurate numbers are difficult to estimate or document statistically because of the illegality of many people's move from the perspective of the receiving countries' entrance rules and regulations. This concerns particularly Europe, North America, Oceania, and certain oil-rich emirates in the Gulf, but also conflict-ridden countries' neighboring areas in Africa, Asia, and the Middle East. Despite the fact that mobility is always gendered, women and men migrate in approximately equal numbers.

Transnationalism and Its Parallel Yet Contradictory Elements

The present essay has two main arguments. The first is that in discussing diasporas and mobility in general, it is important to acknowledge the ways in which they have been both securitized and developmentalized. These two phenomena are actually a two-faceted process with parallel and intertwining but also contradictory strands. While migration is seen as a development resource,[3] 'uncontrolled' population flows—particularly refugees—are looked upon as security threats by states and policy makers, particularly after the events of September 11, 2001. Together, these two strands have politicized the transnational paradigm.

Although the focus of this essay is on phenomena encompassed in the term 'transnationality' (living across borders), it is important to remember that transnationality and diaspora are not mutually exclusive concepts for understanding the mobility-development nexus. The general criteria for a diaspora can be said to be forcible or voluntary dispersal, settlement in multiple locations, and the idea of a homeland. At least in public parlance, the term 'diaspora' homogenizes and essentializes disparate populations through its projection of primordial identities. The very ambiguity as to who is encompassed by the term and the cultural content that constitutes its frame of reference contribute to its political potency. The term itself, however, has no administrative or legal connotations. At the same time, researchers have given the term 'diaspora' multiple interpretations. Since its resurgence in the early 1990s, it has been characterized as a sociological ideal type, as a mode of consciousness or of cultural reproduction, and as a form of social organization. In its broadest definition, the term includes "expatriates, expellees, political refugees, alien residents, immigrants, and ethnic and racial minorities" (Safran 1991: 83). Diasporas can be very heterogeneous along class, ethnic, and gender lines.

In the early 1900s, the term 'transnational' was first used to describe migration (Bourne 1916). An entire literature on transnational business corporations began to appear in the 1970s, at about the same time that scholars of international relations began to use the term (Nye 1976). The term 'transnational' appeared in migration studies in the early 1990s, at approximately the same time that the term 'diaspora' reappeared in scholarship as an analytical category. The transnational paradigm provided an alternative to assimilationist and multiculturalist paradigms to make visible historical and political processes that previous migration paradigms had sometimes obscured. Following the modernization theory, earlier mainstream migration theories assumed migration to be mostly one-directional and determined by push-and-pull factors that migrants were supposed to calculate on a rational, *homo economicus* basis. The transnational migration paradigm does not overlook migrants' economic calculations. Instead, it argues that, rather than push and pull, choices are made in terms of more than one state at the same time and that factors such as nationalism and racism in more than one state also contribute to migrants' multiple, simultaneous connections.

As an analytic lens applied to migrants' lives, transnationality sheds light on simultaneity and bifocality: sending and receiving societies are understood as constituting a single field of analysis. The 'transnational approach' to migration was intended to be a move away from 'methodological nationalism' (Glick Schiller 2003, 2005). The term points to the hegemonic usage of the nation-state as a unit of analysis so that the nation-state is seen as a natural—or at least taken for granted—container of social life (Wimmer and Glick Schiller 2002). Particularly, political science research on migration has been dominated by approaches that place the state at the center of analysis and thus focus on macro-level issues (Piper 2006). Across disciplinary divisions, researchers with a transnational analytical lens have studied identity formation; the economic, political, religious, and socio-cultural practices that migrants engage in; and the impact of these practices on both the sending and receiving country or community. They have suggested typologies to capture variations in the dimensions of transnational migration and have explored the relationship between transnational engagement and assimilation. Whether transnational migration is qualitatively a new

phenomenon or whether it shares similarities with its earlier incarnations has been debated extensively.

   Transnational studies today have numerous subfields;
for example, the topic of transnational families and kinship has developed a trajectory of its own. Most subfields
are separated analytically between the 'ways of being' and
the 'ways of belonging' and approach society as a border-
crossing social field (Glick Schiller 2003). In the writings
of Nina Glick Schiller and her co-authors, the idea of
social fields is based more on the Manchester School's
view of anthropology than on Pierre Bourdieu's work: in
a transnational approach to migration, this concept refers
to an egocentric 'network of networks' (Levitt and Glick
Schiller 2004). Transnational social fields are a set of multiple interlocking networks of social relationships through
which ideas, practices, and resources are unequally
exchanged, organized, and transformed (ibid.). However,
Glick Schiller (this volume) points out that the migration
scholars who have theorized transnational social fields
have seen them as linking mechanisms through which
migrants become incorporated in two or more nation-
states. Thus, the critique of methodological nationalism
did not lead most migration scholars who have theorized
transnational social fields to an advocacy of 'methodological individualism' in a similar vein as in the parallel trend
of network analysis. The state and social institutions are
not erased from the domain of analysis.

   The second main argument of this text is that the politicization of the transnational paradigm and the neo-liberal
mega-trend are in practice entwined, despite the fact
that when transnationalism was introduced to migration
research, it was part of a critique of uneven development
and capitalist exploitation of labor. In fact, Basch, Glick
Schiller, and Blanc (1994) warned in *Nations Unbound*
of the likelihood that the concept would be utilized for

neo-liberal political purposes. Transnational studies have achieved considerable, yet contested and partially indirect, paradigmatic power. Development and security have been brought together and separated by major international actors, such as the United Nations and the European Union, in discourses and practices that concern migration and refugees. This essay discusses these trends from the viewpoint of transnationality in order to bring the increased role of security concerns and its implications for a transnational paradigm to the attention of migration scholars.

Interest in transnational migration grows steadily among international development stakeholders and actors. The European Commission's Official Consensus on Development in March 2006 devoted approximately three sentences to mobility, two sentences to migrant remittances, and one sentence to 'brain drain'. In the summer of 2007, the European Commission announced its intention to establish a European Migration Network that would produce up-to-date information about migration and refugees and would aim to bring together key persons, experts, and decision makers. In addition to its principal documents, the World Bank has started to publish *Migration and Development Briefs*. Migration is the theme of the most recent report of the United Nations High Commissioner for Refugees (UNDP 2009).

I suggest that this developmentalization of mobility is not merely a consequence of the contemporary forces of capitalist restructuring but is as much related to the securitization of mobility. Neither the connection between development and international migration nor that between security (approached in this essay primarily through the topics of conflicts and wars) and people's mobility is novel. On the one hand, early migration researchers who followed modernization theory regarded economic reasons—with regard to both migrants and receiving countries—as the driving force behind migration. On the other hand, huge refugee movements were also a familiar phenomenon in Europe in the aftermath of World War II. This led to the 1951 United Nations Convention Relating to the Status of Refugees, which agreed upon three preferred solutions for such situations: return at the earliest possible stage, compensation, and resettlement in a new country (which could be a third country, rather than the country of first asylum). These three options can be regarded as the 'international refugee regime'. Whereas the two latter options are not mutually exclusive, the last provides access to new citizenship and the termination of refugee status.

Development, security, and mobility have thus been interrelated for a long time but what is novel for the scholarship of transnational mobility is the changed relationship of meanings of these terms. Securitization does not always, or only, mean militarization. The hierarchy between development and security in the context of migrant and refugee mobility changed in the post–Cold War context, at least in receiving countries' considerations. The contemporary restrictive trend toward refugee mobility, which I will elaborate on throughout this essay in its relation to 'new humanitarianism', became visible in Europe in the late 1990s, when the 'threat' of a massive flight of ethnic Albanian refugees from Kosovo was seen as justification for the NATO air war toward Serbia and Kosovo on humanitarian terms. This change regarding the ways in which migration is understood in relationship to development and security cannot be separated from economics. However, the fact that migration is now a part of security policies rather than development practices, or that development practices that touch upon mobility are drafted primarily in security conditions, is striking.

Based on analyses of security understandings of the United Nations (Hammerstad 2000; Owen 2008; Slim 2001), of European Union migration policies (Ceccorulli 2009;

Peltonen 2007; Piper 2006), and of the European security strategy (Ceccorulli 2009; Kaldor 2007), I suggest that the promotion of development 'back home' in the developing world—and also in acute conflict areas—is now being used as a pretext to justify security practices in the context of mobility. Put bluntly, in terms of development assistance and humanitarian aid (including humanitarian interventions), the promotion of practices that restrict migrant and refugee mobility is, from the rich migrant-receiving countries' viewpoint, regarded as a kind of 'pre-emptive self-defense'. This approach characterized the Bush administration's rhetoric on and practices of a 'global war on terror'. Thus, a 'global approach on migration', as the term is used in EU policy (Ceccorulli 2009), and a 'new humanitarianism' (Slim 2001) are intertwined in relation to migration and refugeeness. Migrants (along with the remittances that they are expected to send) and refugees are at the center of the relationship between development and security. Conceptually, this interdependency is operationalized in terms such as 'human security' and 'mixed migratory flows'.

Interpretations among political actors, including the Organisation for Economic Co-operation and Development (OECD) and its Development Assistance Committee (DAC), the European Union Commission, and international financial institutions such as the World Bank and the International Monetary Fund (IMF), about how and what kind of border-crossing lifestyles benefit the developing countries while preventing secondary movements of refugees and illegal migration to the West have incorporated a transnational paradigm into neo-liberal development strategies and policies.[4] One could mention assistance in the region of origin, development through local integration for refugee populations, and the acceptance, even promotion, of transnational relations as an enduring, if not durable, solution for refugee problems (see, e.g., Ceccorulli 2009; Stepputat 2004; Van Hear 2002). These assistance modes, which aim to improve refugees' self-reliance and move away from reactive 'care and concern', are not negative as such. The problem is, however, that the above-mentioned models are applied in top-down frameworks, with the additional goal of curtailing migrants' and refugees' freedom of movement. Hence, 'mobile livelihoods'[5] are increasingly instrumentalized and forged from 'above'. Transnational practices that do not fit the political projects promoted within the 'accepted' transnational relations are in danger of becoming either forbidden or very vulnerable.

Transnationality and 'New Wars': Mobility and Security with Reference to the Individual

Transnationalism as a theoretical entry point to mobility emerged parallel to other theories that aimed to build on networks in the post–Cold War political context in which major changes in security understandings were underway. In this section, I discuss the meaning of concepts such as 'human security' and 'new wars' as they apply to policies toward refugees and migrants. I start by briefly reviewing the history of the political associations between security and refugee mobility. Then I discuss how refugees and security have been brought together in the United Nations, which is the most important international organization responsible for refugee security. The aim of this section is to demonstrate how conflict-generated mobility has become the most important indicator of the lack of security. Because what policy makers call mixed migratory flows accompany the global restructuring of capitalist production, the view on refugee mobility as an indicator of insecurity has boiled down to restrictive politics toward migration in general.

Mobility and Security Considerations: A Brief Overview

For a period longer than migration as such, states have viewed refugee mobility as a political and security issue that requires international agreements. According to Loescher and Milner (2005: 23), international political concern for the fate of refugees first emerged after World War I, when massive refugee flows resulting from the break-up of the Habsburg, Hohenzollern, Ottoman, and Romanov empires in Europe, Turkey, the Middle East, and Russia and from the Russian Civil War, the Polish-Soviet War, and the Russian famine of 1921 heightened inter-state tensions and threatened the security of European countries. Consequently, an international framework of institutions and agreements was created in 1921 within the League of Nations. Following World War II, the current international refugee regime, which was described at the outset of this essay, emerged in reaction to the security threat posed by some 12 million displaced persons, mainly from Eastern and Central Europe and the Soviet Union. While millions were repatriated or resettled in the aftermath of the war, nearly 500,000 remained in camps in Western Europe until the mid-1960s (ibid.).

During the Cold War, the political and security perspective on refugees was universal: they were seen as part of the struggle between the East and the West. In regions of intense superpower conflict and competition, refugees were armed, and their military struggles were supported materially and ideologically. Throughout the Cold War, refugees and the safety problems they raised were considered to be part of a wider set of geo-political considerations, including an understanding that most threats to a state's security were military, arising from outside its borders, and required a political or military response. Thus, while specific refugee groups were perceived as assets or liabilities during times of crisis, the security logic was bound by a highly constrained notion of security that did not see migration as a central issue (Loescher and Milner 2005: 24).

The view on migration and its importance in safety considerations changed in the post–Cold War era when the security implications of forced migration gained more salience (Loescher and Milner 2005). The United Nations became the central arena for voicing these altered security understandings: in a changed political situation, the most powerful member countries felt free to declare that they did not want refugees and considered them a burden (Hammerstad 2000; Slim 2001). Moreover, the large-scale displacement of civilian populations became a deliberate conflict strategy in places such as, for example, the Balkans, sub-Saharan Africa, and East Timor. There was a common recognition among the states (particularly in Europe and North America) that refugee movements not only were a consequence of insecurity but also could be a cause of instability for host states, countries of origin, and regions in conflict—and could even pose a threat to wider international peace and security. As a result of intra-state conflicts in the Middle East, the Balkans, the Caucasus, Africa, and elsewhere, the security implications of refugee movements began to dominate political developments at the United Nations Security Council, NATO, and other security organizations (Loescher and Milner 2005: 24).

In the late 1980s and the 1990s, a dramatic change took place in international norms on state sovereignty and non-intervention as a consequence of 'new wars', which produced massive refugee flows and internal displacement. Resulting from the emergence of the so-called global humanitarian regime that I elaborate on below in the context of security understandings in the United Nations, the 1990s is also known as the decade of humanitarian interventions. Mary Kaldor (2007: 3–4; italics added) defines 'new wars' as network wars in a way that demonstrates the link between the politicization of the transnational paradigm and the current thinking on security:

> '[N]ew wars' … take place in the context of the disintegration of states (typically authoritarian states under the impact of globalization). They are fought by networks of state and non-state actors … most violence is directed against civilians … taxation is falling and war finance consists of loot and pillage, illegal trading and other war-generated revenue … the distinctions between combatant and non-combatant, legitimate violence and criminality are all breaking down … Above all, they construct new sectarian identities (religious, ethnic or tribal) that undermine the sense of a shared political community. Indeed, this could be considered the purpose of these wars. They recreate the sense of political community along new divisive lines through the manufacture of fear and hate … Moreover, these sectarian political identities are often inextricably tied to criminalized networks that provide a basis for a *global shadow economy* … 'new wars' are very difficult to end … *they tend to spread through refugees and displaced persons, criminalized networks*, and the sectarian ideologies they manufacture.

Loescher and Milner, who aim to "bring into the mainstream of international relations and security studies an understanding of strategic roots and consequences of refugee movements" (Loescher 1992: 3), suggest that, from the mid-1990s up to the present day, writings on migration and security in security studies, political science, and sociology have focused on the securitization of asylum in the European context (Loescher and Milner 2005: 25).

Debates about asylum, immigration, social identity, and cohesion have been translated into state action against asylum seekers and migrants. The main discourses of this discussion have been integration and assimilation rather than transnationality.

Security concerns have heightened since the events of September 11 and the subsequent US-led 'global war on terror'. The new security agenda has sharpened the association for many Western security and policy analysts—but also for some social scientists—between refugees, asylum seekers, and illegal migrants, on the one hand, and the issue of insecurity, on the other. During the current decade, there has been an emphasis on the potential links between migration and asylum in the West and transnational crime, terrorism (see, e.g., Brouwer, Catz, and Guild 2003; EUPOL 2009; European Union 2003), national identity, and societal security. In the European Union, improving the border management of adjoining states and regions and controlling illegal migration and trafficking have become top priorities for policy makers and, as a result, have led to a politics of regionalism (Ceccorulli 2009). Western policy makers increasingly believe that the potential security threats of refugee movements can be contained in regions of refugee origin. The implications of this approach produce a binary opposition between human rights and security ideology, a paradox that is embedded in the ways that the United Nations talks about refugees and deals with their issues.

Humanitarian Interventions: Preventing and Containing Refugee Movements

Humanitarianism is not inherently a pacifist ideology (see, e.g., Slim 2001). In the late 1990s, B. S. Chimini (2000: 2), a specialist on international legislation concerning refugees, argued that "humanitarianism is *the* ideology of hegemonic states in the era of globalization [and this] ideology of humanitarianism mobilises a large range of meanings and practices to establish and sustain global relations of domination." Hugo Slim (2001: 331–332) explains that "humanitarian action can extend from infant-feeding and water supply through economic sanctions and peace-keeping to the use of force, and then beyond to peace-building activities, state repair and democratization." He talks about the construction of what he refers to as 'violent humanitarianism' in the 1990s and traces the foundation of a new form of interventionist and militarized agenda in the United Nations to a report, titled *An Agenda for Peace*, of then UN Secretary-General Boutros-Ghali (1992). The report reflected the emergence of the issue of security in the United Nations debates and the inclusion of refugees into the security discourse. It renewed the right and the intention of the United Nations to use force (referred to as 'preventive deployment') if all other means failed (as per Article 42 of Chapter VII of the United Nations Charter). The paragraphs below and the argumentation of this essay in general show that humanitarian interventions have often been conducted primarily to prevent refugee crises or at least to contain them in the areas of conflict and have thereby contributed to the politicization of the transnational paradigm.

The United Nations, Refugees, and Security

States have been prompted for reasons of national and regional security to tackle the problem of human displacement in a more preventive manner, addressing the conditions which force people to abandon their homes. (UNHCR 1996–1997)

The United Nations High Commissioner for Refugees (UNHCR) was founded by the United Nations General Assembly in 1950 with the statutory responsibility to provide international protection to refugees and to seek permanent solutions to their problems. During the Cold War, its activities were two-fold: in the developed world, it worked to ensure that states hosting refugees from communist countries adhered to their international legal obligations according to the 1951 refugees convention; in the developing world, it maintained refugee camps in the borders adjoining protracted superpower proxy wars, such as those in Afghanistan and Angola. Presently, its primary focus has shifted from providing international protection for refugees to managing large-scale humanitarian operations that assist war-affected populations in the midst of conflicts (Goodwin-Gill 1999; Hammerstad 2000). According to Anne Hammerstad (2000), this operational transformation was accompanied by a significant conceptual change in the 1990s that involved a re-evaluation of the nature of refugee emergencies and of the UNHCR's own role in dealing with them.

As described in the previous section, changes took place in the late 1980s and the 1990s in the operational environment as the political stance on refugees changed in the West. Rich countries, especially those in Europe, wanted increasingly to deter refugees and asylum seekers from crossing their borders. The reasons were many: migrants, including refugees, were no longer welcomed as workers due to a decrease in demand and an increase in supply; xenophobic right-wing parties with anti-immigration policies became more popular; and refugees were no longer ideological trump cards in the global struggle between the East and the West. During this same period, the number of refugees rose sharply as a result of conflicts in the Balkans and East Timor and due to the Rwandan genocide. In this changed political context, Western states began to employ policies that mirrored their interest in restricting refugee flows. They undertook humanitarian actions and military humanitarian interventions to contain potential refugees within their countries or regions of origin. Moreover, both the states and the UNHCR have, to an increasing extent, sought to repatriate refugees at the earliest possible stage, which has sometimes led to forced repatriation (Hammerstad 2000: 393).

The operational change of the UNHCR that reflected the altered policies of its donor countries was the development of a security discourse within the refugee agency in the 1990s. According to Hammerstad (2000: 395), the traditional focus of the UNHCR on the legal and human rights and humanitarian needs of refugee individuals and on the corresponding international legal obligations of the states was not entirely replaced but rather became gradually subsumed within the security discourse. In a keynote speech at a ministerial meeting on human security issues in Bergen, Norway, the then UN High Commissioner for Refugees, Sadako Ogata (1999), claimed that the first aim of the United Nations Charter is to maintain "international peace and security" with the goal of achieving "human security" and named refugees as a "significant symptom" of the insecurities of the post–Cold War world (cf. Hammerstad 2000: 396). Hence, the UNHCR's discourse on refugees legitimizes the new security paradigm by explaining that refugee flows must be prevented, contained, and reversed because of the security threats that they create for the social cohesion, political integrity, and economic welfare of host states, for regional and international stability, for humanitarian workers, and for the refugees themselves (ibid.).

The term 'human security' is an ambiguous and broad concept that is employed extensively to conceptualize the security discourse in the United Nations and some other international organizations, such as the Organization for Security and Co-operation in Europe (OSCE). Yet its future in the United Nations as well as among other international actors is far from certain. For instance, in his report, *In Larger Freedom*, then UN Secretary-General Kofi Annan (2005) uses the term only once, speaking more often of a concept of 'collective security' (see also Owen 2008: 119). In the United Nations, the notion of human security was first promulgated by the United Nations Development Programme (UNDP 1993): "Security should be interpreted as security for people, not security for land ... The concept of security must change—from an exclusive stress on national security to much greater stress on people's security, from security through armaments, to security through human development, from territorial security to food, employment and environmental security." The UNDP's (1994) *Human Development Report* identified core elements that together made up the idea of human security: economic security, food security, health security, personal security, community security, and political security. The human security approach has since developed in two main directions, one emphasizing security in the face of political violence (freedom from fear and freedom from want), the other emphasizing the interrelatedness of different types of security and the particular importance of development as a security strategy.

Taylor Owen (2008: 120) argues that the Secretary-General and many member states are reluctant to endorse fully the concept of human security because of the United Nations' conflation of state security and human development and the overlap between human security and human rights. Even if some United Nations' documents, such as

Human Security Now (Ogata and Sen 2003), stress that human security is a complementary rather than a competing paradigm to national security (see Owen 2008: 118), the obvious reason for many member states' reluctance to endorse human security is that they acknowledge the potential conflicts between the security of the individual, the political community, and state borders. Especially in matters of strategic importance, states are unwilling to be exposed to challenges to their own sovereignty, although they may challenge other states that are considered 'fragile', 'rogue', or 'failed'. A "certain reluctance at supranationalization" with regard to migration as a security threat is evident even in the European Union (Ceccorulli 2009: 7).

For Owen (2008), human security is a precondition for human development, but not vice versa: human security looks directly at the threat outcomes, such as violence or economic downturns, while development looks at the empowerment process. Human development is more concerned with long-term institution building, whereas human security addresses emergency relief. The focus on emergencies is linked to the 'responsibility to protect' slogan that is used to justify 'humanitarian interventions' in the sense that links human security to the protection of human rights: if the state is dysfunctional, then international organizations must step in, not just to pressure the state to respect human rights, but to assume the state's duty to protect (ibid.: 121). A neo-liberal vein became visible in the report of the Trade and Development Board of the United Nations (2005: 4), which separates development from peace and security in relation to the international community's obligations, stating that "each country must take primary responsibility for its own development and that the role of national policies and development strategies cannot be overemphasized in the achievement of sustainable development" (cf. Owen 2008: 120).

Human Security in EU Policies:
Security-Centered Mobility Awareness and Its Implications for Development

While the European Union is trying to build 'Fortress Europe', the OSCE has been adopting the phrase 'human security' in its vocabulary. This became evident in the European Union's (2003) security strategy report, *A Secure Europe in a Better World*. Mary Kaldor (2007: 182–183), who is the principal academic voice of the new security doctrine of the OSCE, suggests that human security potentially offers a new approach to both security and development. While this strategy is new in comparison to the narrowly state-centered, violence-based approaches, associations between peace and development are not solely contemporary; rather, they can be traced, scholarly and philosophically, to the work of Immanuel Kant, preceding the concept of human security by centuries. The essence of the so-called liberal peace theory is that democracies do not go to war with each other (e.g., Turner 2006).

From methodological and theoretical angles, it is the emphasis on individuals that seems to form the continuum between different peace development associations. For instance, Adam Curle (1971: 174) identified development as a possibility of individual capacity building to be one of the key components of peace building through the restructuring of conflicting relationships from below. The empowerment of an individual and her or his capabilities are also at the center of Nobel-awarded economist Amartya Sen's thinking on human security, which constitutes the foundation of the UNDP core understanding of human security. The fact that the human security concept has been brought to the UNHCR security thinking from the United Nations Development Programme shows again the close interrelation among development, security, and migration.

With regard to an understanding of 'new wars', human security, and the transnational paradigm, what is common among them is that they all move away from methodological nationalism.[6] Thus, methodological individualism, a conceptual if not operational focus on people rather than on borders, is perhaps the prevailing factor that led policy makers to use transnationality as an entry point to mobility in the context of 'global governance' and 'global humanitarian regime'. One implication of human security policy is the intertwining of humanitarian and development assistance (Kaldor 2007: 193). In the context of 'new wars', underdevelopment is seen as a security threat and as a source of social unrest.

When the human security approach is operationalized in terms of the West and of security organizations such as OSCE, NATO, and the United Nations Security Council, its human rights potential is ambivalent. When state security and individual or community security are in real or alleged contradiction, the dispute is also political. When it comes to controlling mobility, the protection of state borders may become one of the primary components of maintaining the human security of some populations or individuals. In most developed countries, refugees and immigrants do not threaten state security but are increasingly considered as threats to different aspects of their citizens' human security.[7] Thus, the relationship between human security and human rights is not straightforward.

Underdevelopment, as a source of social unrest and conflict, and natural catastrophes produce 'uncontrolled' mobility, which is unwanted in terms of Western immigration and refugee policies. The association between migration and security has upgraded migration management to a strategic matter of top priority in the European Union. The interest in controlling unwanted inflows of migrants has an impact on the European Union's external relations

and mingles with its other core policy fields (Ceccorulli
2009: 2). For policy makers, the fact that people live their
lives through different categories such as 'displaced',
'refugee', and 'economic migrant' and that countries
seldom produce only one kind of movers has produced
the problem of mixed migratory flows. In essence, policy
makers confront problems of governance and center their
concerns on what they see as the potential danger of
abuse to a system that is, in principle, based on human
rights and international legislation on refugees. In 2003,
the European Commission noted that the "[a]buse of
asylum procedures is on the rise, as are mixed migratory
flows, often maintained by smuggling practices involving both people with a legitimate need for international
protection and migrants using asylum procedures to gain
access to the member states to improve their living conditions."[8] This rhetoric, which on the surface compartmen-
talizes different kinds of mobility, highlights interestingly
how policy makers label mobility selectively in an era
of security-centered, development-oriented, and, in its
aspirations, rights-based humanitarianism. Following this
trend, the current UNHCR documents (see, e.g., UNHCR
2009) have added 'mixed migration populations' to their
vocabulary and use the expression matter-of-factly.

The term 'asylum migrant' is used negatively in the
context of migrants who enter Europe and other Western
countries illegally. In practice, it points to a mobility that
fits well in 'guest worker' regimes that are re-emerging
in the West in the guise of 'circular migration' (see Glick
Schiller, this volume; Piper 2006). Asylum migrants are
people who will most likely fail to achieve asylum but
will, in the meantime, send remittances to their families
while working in the economy's exploitative gray sector.
Thus, different regimes and categories that are discussed
in terms of humanitarian and security concerns cannot

be separated from an analysis of the fluctuating needs of the labor market and the current preference for short-term temporary workers who have no rights with regard to entitlements, settlement, or family reunification.

The fear of abuse to the system is slightly ironic in the face of the fact that there seem to be processes under way that burden migrants and refugees with responsibilities that used to belong to states and the international community in terms of post-conflict reconstruction, assistance toward refugees, and development. Some attempts to replace political solutions to the refugee crisis with a technical 'hands on' approach and aspects of moving from relief assistance to a development mode of assistance have a potential of working either toward 'transnationalism from above' or 'transnationalism from below'. There is potential for the former in the promotion of transnational relations that are restricted by the rich countries to the refugees' region of origin. It suggests that refugees are seen as integrated diasporas that enhance positive development in the conflict area while remaining in its immediate vicinity, instead of moving to the European Union or other rich countries.

Hence, globally, state officials' consciousness of mobility is kept on permanent alert. 'Comprehensive border awareness' packages are sold to states (including, recently, Qatar and Estonia) by private security companies, such as the European Aeronautic Defence and Space Company (EADS),[9] and the fences and high-tech surveillance equipment outside Ceuta and Melilla are intended to block sub-Saharan and West African migrants and asylum seekers from entering the Schengen Area. Countries such as Senegal, Mali, Mauritania, and Morocco receive substantial amounts of development assistance from the European Union and from Spain on the condition that they commit themselves to restricting the border crossing of their populations (Peltonen 2007). These extreme preventive policies and measures have unintentionally increased illegal mobility to the Canary Islands, continental Spain, and Italy (ibid.). The methodological individualism of human security as applied to mobility does not in effect lessen the emphasis on borders.

Controlling mixed migration populations takes many forms. For example, the European Union has a Strategic Committee on Immigration, Frontiers and Asylum (SCIFA) that also works in cooperation with external partners. The United States expects the European Union's cooperation with border control in transit areas, border information exchange, return of inadmissible persons, and so forth. The focus is on individuals who cross borders with the goal being "to obtain information about those crossing frontiers and ensure maximum security" (van Selm and Tsolakis 2004: 8; cf. Ceccorulli 2009: 11). The strategic security emphasis on mobility that is illegal in the face of EU rules and regulations is a continuous trend. The renewed focus on illegal immigration can be found in the European Union's (2008) *Report on the Implementation of the European Security Strategy: Providing Security in a Changing World* (cf. Ceccorulli 2009: 10).

In general, the official criteria for current development assistance (e.g., that of the European Union) are needs and performance. The latter indicates that the aid is conditional: it is linked to the human rights regime. In the context of wars and conflicts, as well as post-conflict reconstruction, some analysts suggest that such aid seeks a complete transformation of a society's values and behavioral patterns (see, e.g., Duffield 2001). This development intervention, which is sometimes preceded by and combined with military intervention that is justified in humanitarian terms, can be explained by the donor community's belief in the liberal peace theory that I elaborated on earlier. Such an aid regime is characterized by institution building, a rights-based approach, and what Dezalay and Garth (2002) refer to as 'legal globalization'—that is, the transnationalization of legal models, frameworks, and ideas. However, despite the fact that such aid makes reference to human rights and democracy, the transnational dimensions of these aid relations (even outside the military context) are not necessarily democratic. For example, in many aid-receiving developing countries, democratic elections do not take place until after structural adjustment programs initiated by the IMF and the World Bank have been implemented (Duffield 2001). This implementation is often conducted by so-called contractor states,[10] with much of the multi-level aid surpassing Third World governments or embryonic state structures due to the central role given to both non-governmental organizations (NGOs) and international non-governmental organizations (INGOs). These organizations are sub-contracted aid distributors, as well as important aid recipients.

Migrant remittances and diaspora investments are important survival instruments in societies undergoing structural adjustment programs, while the same programs produce migration flows linked to specific First World labor needs, such as care work in an aging Europe. Remittance-migration formations also appear in areas of conflict and high levels of internal violence. Consider, for example, female migration from Central and South American states such as Bolivia and Colombia to Spain and Italy, which is triggered by high levels of internal violence and, more often than not, the dissolution of conjugal ties (Sørensen 2005). Sometimes family dissolution happens as a consequence of structural adjustment programs that cause gendered unemployment, preventing men from providing for their families—an important notion of masculinity in several societies. As a result, many women are abandoned, and some of them migrate. Migration and refugeeness are at the center of the development-security nexus, and many variations of the transnationality theme are manifestations of this connection. Paradoxically, while the centrality of transnational mobility for the development-security nexus is visible, it is not 'seen' in the writings of most anthropologists working within the transnational paradigm. Perhaps this is because this connection allegedly belongs to the realm of development, the "evil twin" of anthropology (Ferguson 1997).

A Transnational Approach to Migration Policies: Remittances

Bilateral and multilateral development agencies have increasingly stressed that remittances play an important role in the survival of poor individuals, families, and communities around the world. Policy discussions on migration have undergone some changes during the last two decades or so. Throughout the 1990s, the European Commission and other policy interlocutors in international thinking and at state levels promoted the idea that migration and refugee flows should be reduced by generating local development, preventing and resolving local conflicts, and retaining refugees in neighboring or first countries of asylum. This approach, commonly labeled 'combating the root causes of migration' (see Ceccorulli 2009; Sørensen 2004), achieved its structural limits during the late 1990s, when research demonstrated that an increase in economic productivity may simultaneously increase mobility, at least in the short term. This was referred to as the 'migration hump'. The term pointed to the paradox that the same economic policies that can reduce migration in the long term can increase it in the short term (Pastore 2003; cf. Sørensen 2004). It is important to note that because of the general securitization trend and the current economic downturn, the strategy of combating the root causes of migration has not disappeared: it is the principal policy guideline of most United Nations and European Union documents on migration.

The transnational approach was explicitly brought to the development policy arena at the turn of the millennium. This method sees internal, regional, and international mobility as an intrinsic dimension of development and views mobility as an essential condition for economic and social development (Sørensen 2004). For example, the World Bank and the DAC began to encourage diasporas to become engaged in positive development roles in their countries of origin. In 2003, the World Bank's Global Development Finance Report took formal notice of remittances as a source of external development finance for the first time, and UN Secretary-General Annan identified migration as a priority issue for the international community. Estimated at around US \$283 billion in 2008 (Ratha, Mohapatra, and Xu 2008), registered remittances to developing countries represent a large proportion of global financial flows, and there is reason to believe that substantial amounts remain unregistered. Based on available evidence, various reports estimate that remittances amount to more than double the official assistance, which is more than capital market flows and more than half of foreign direct investment flows to development countries, despite the fact that in real terms remittances were expected to fall from 2 percent of GDP in 2007 to 1.8 in 2008 (ibid.).

According to Ninna Nyberg Sørensen (2004), what underlies the development dimension of migrant transfers is that remittances are said to have the potential of being more stable than private capital flows and to be less vulnerable to changing economic cycles—an aspect that has been emphasized in the migration and development literature. While it is true that remittances have some degree of regularity because of the ongoing family and kinship ties that motivate them, migrants are not immune to changes in the economy. On the contrary, they are primarily positioned in economic niches that are the most vulnerable to market changes. Almost all migrants—from highly educated and well-paid professionals to workers in the construction industry, care work, and service work— share this vulnerability to economic downturns. Sometimes remitting persons do not have work permits, which means that they do not pay taxes. But it also means that they are not covered by legislation that protects workers in the workplace and cannot take advantage of membership in trade unions. Nor do they not have the safety net of unemployment benefits in times of economic decline.

The discourse on remittances and development not only neglects the vulnerability of migrant workers in the workplace, but also fails to examine the effect of violent conflict on transnational relations and remittance flows. In the context of violence, the importance of mobility as a resource increases. Yet increasingly conflict-generated diaspora members in the West and their transnational connections are not screened through international legislation on refugees. Instead, they are examined through the lens of the 'global war on terror' (for operational measures, see, e.g., Ceccorulli 2009: 11) and accused of spreading 'new wars' to the cities of the West by replicating confrontational bifurcations in the new settings, committing terrorist acts, and perpetuating conflicts 'back home' through 'long-distance nationalism', that is, different kinds of remittances. 'Home-grown' terrorism by second-generation immigrants is a growing concern in Europe (EUPOL 2009), and security-oriented literature, policy papers, and journalistic writings on this subject are abundant. As much as the slogan 'responsibility to protect' has become a constituent of humanitarian interventions and peace enforcement, the First World countries' popular attitude is that politicians and lawmakers should protect citizens from refugees and, to a lesser extent, migrants. Perhaps that is why, instead of transnationality, multiculturalism and integration remain the main discourses concerning the migrant and refugee presence in the West within the larger question of security. Multiculturalism and integration are used both as analytical frameworks and as policy guidelines. Keeping in mind the earlier cited definition of 'new wars', I would argue that multiculturalism and integration can be seen more as manifestations of the deep politicization and securitization of transnational mobility than as adequate theoretical tools for social science and migration studies.

Migration studies have examined the different ways that migrants remit and how remittances influence community development, economic structures, and relations between genders and family members. This literature has drawn attention to migrants' economic contributions and has probably increased policy makers' interest in migrants' role in the development of the sending countries. Several migrant-sending countries have taken formal notice of the importance of remittances, introducing laws and other channels to facilitate remitting and to support migrant investments. To maintain their loyalty, sending countries treat migrants as important constituents of the nation and give them special rights, such as an expatriate vote and dual citizenship. While states are simultaneously forging and institutionalizing transnational relations and lifestyles, the migrants' transnational activities can threaten the stability of migrant- and refugee-sending countries when members of diasporas engage in political lobbying, opposition politics, and separatist and terrorist movements.

The self-help component of remittances can also be destabilizing on an individual level. Because remittances are often sent to individuals, they can be a source of conflict and friction within transnational families and communities. Migration and transnationality can—and in many cases do—increase inequality. Sometimes they contribute to hierarchical gender relations and other inequities among those who stayed behind. In this regard, migrant remittances reflect the neo-liberal order of the day, which is built on competitive and consumption-oriented individualism. Policies cannot be divorced from politics. Put together with the promotion of the role of transnational relations in enhancing development 'back home', this is one of the points where the transnational paradigm meets neo-liberal economics.

Sedentary Regimes and Transnational Solutions?

In the 1950s, the United Nations forged an international refugee regime, based on three 'durable' solutions for refugee crises: integration in the first country of asylum, resettlement in a third country, or repatriation (i.e., return to the home country) at the earliest possible date. The last continues to be seen as the best and most 'natural' option. However, since the 1990s (note the timing), it has been increasingly admitted that return is not an easy or simple 'optimal solution' (see, e.g., Koser and Black 1999). Anthropologists such as Liisa Malkki and Laura Hammond have criticized this international refugee regime for its sedentary thinking, in the sense that people were being conceptualized as naturally rooted in the soil. This critique is also part of the UNHCR's (1995) effort to move from a "reactive, exile-oriented and refugee-specific" approach toward one that is "proactive, homeland-oriented and holistic" and, according to Van Hear (2002), includes acknowledging refugee crises as transnational phenomena.

But what does this recognition actually mean? In essence, it means that policy makers recognize that refugee crises are transnational problems and act accordingly in line with their own security, development, and economic considerations. According to Hammerstad (2000: 396), the UNHCR's approach "emphasizes the prevention and containment of refugee flows and advocates conflict resolution, reconstruction and refugee repatriation." Heterogeneous types of mobility are inherently seen as people out of place. This is signaled by the use of sedentary concepts such as displaced persons and IDP (internally displaced people). In her agenda for human security, Kaldor (2007: 183) asserts: "Perhaps the indicator that comes closest to a measure of human security is displaced persons. Displaced persons are a typical feature of contemporary crises, both natural disasters and wars. There has been a steady increase in the number of displaced persons per conflict over the last decades ... Displaced persons are the victims of both physical and material insecurity."

The above citation ties mobility and human security tightly together, making mobility an indicator of a lack of security, the idea being that people do not leave their homes and communities unless they are faced with a serious threat (see, e.g., UNHCR 1997). Moreover, reflecting the conceptual transformation among international organizations and states on security, mobility, and the obligations stated in international refugee legislation, it shows clearly that the discourse on crisis-generated mobility is increasingly that of displaced persons rather than refugees. The reasons for this shift are several. While the contemporary numbers of IDP are higher than refugee figures, my estimation is that the balance would shift if the crossing of international borders, which is the main legal condition of the definition 'refugee', was less restricted. Besides, while the concept 'refugee' implies legal rights and protection provided by the international community and individual states alike, 'displaced person' is merely a descriptive term that does not denote any rights or entitlements.

Development assistance for refugees (DAR) programs have been reinvented to revitalize local integration as a durable solution for refugee problems in order to limit the secondary movement of refugees from countries of first asylum and mixed flows of refugees and migrants toward the European Union and other rich regions (Stepputat 2004: 18). Whether these programs have actually been successful in the conflict areas and have improved refugees' lives varies case by case. What is more relevant here is how these programs forge mobility precisely because they acknowledge the refugee crisis as a transnational phenomenon: their aim is to restrict refugees from moving and to advocate support for refugee-hosting areas. DAR aims to strengthen the self-reliance of refugees and thereby increase their contribution to local development, decrease the need for long-term care and maintenance programs, reduce the potential for host-refugee conflicts, and better prepare refugees for durable solutions 'through development' (ibid.). Behind these models seems also to be evidence of the so-called windmill effect. The term suggests that after the initial crisis, the refugee presence boosts the local economy by increasing the capacity to utilize natural resources and by creating new niches in the labor market (see, for example, Van Hear 1998).

Although many refugees are desperate to return home as soon as possible and, sometimes more importantly, regain access to farmable land and their property, not all people who flee are willing to return to the place of departure. Past experiences can be extremely traumatic, and donor-driven 'truth and reconciliation' processes or former fighters' reintegration programs often fail to address the unresolved atrocities (see, e.g., Rosen 2007). This is particularly evident in the so-called minority returns. Post-conflict circumstances are sometimes characterized by a tradition of impunity.

Development and Post-conflict Return

In the following paragraphs, I will reflect on the discussion of Sørensen, Van Hear, and Engberg-Pedersen (2003) regarding post-conflict return and development. The empirical cue for this analysis draws from my own ethnographic data about Palestinian return migrants.[11] In terms of development, Sørensen, Van Hear, and Engberg-Pedersen suggest that migrants' return to the home country after a short period abroad is not likely to contribute to development, especially if the movement is abrupt. They also suggest that the return after a longer stay abroad has much greater development potential.

My ethnographic case data among Palestinian returnees provide some evidence of this trend, but also suggest that the degree to which returnees contribute to development reflects on where and in what conditions they have spent their time abroad. Whether or not they were refugees by legal status did not much matter. Perhaps more importantly for the present argument, my material suggests that sometimes people returned because of the development potential of a place that had been defined as a post-conflict site by the international donor community. For example, migrants who returned to the West Bank and Gaza Strip in the optimistic 'days of Oslo' had no idea that post-conflict reconstruction assistance programs and investments are usually short-term. Some had returned in an optimistic vein without considerable economic resources of their

own, while some had no choice except to return. As often
happens in post-conflict situations where the root causes
of the hostilities have not been resolved, the Palestine-
Israel conflict re-escalated, and thus development in the
occupied Palestinian territory turned to de-development
and arrested state building.

Moreover, Sørensen, Van Hear, and Engberg-Pedersen
(2003) note that states with a history of violent conflict
are more willing to encourage refugees to contribute
resources from abroad rather than to return and participate
directly in the post-conflict nation-state building process.
The argument of the authors that a state in-the-making or
recovering from a conflict may prefer that at least certain
segments of diaspora remain abroad is valid also in light
of my ethnographic material. Rather than encouraging
migrants or refugees to return, which would burden the
fragile infrastructure and peace, the state leadership often
hopes that they will invest from abroad. These states may
not welcome returnees if their move to the former home
country is intended to be one-directional and if they arrive
with expectations of a welfare state or long-term international assistance after their return. Thus, in contrast to the
expectations of the international refugee regime, the pref-
erences of those who stayed in the home country and the
policies of post-conflict societies may discourage migrants'
and refugees' permanent return to the homeland.

The forces that encourage remittances and investments
from abroad but discourage return engender a further set
of questions about remittances and the security of both
individuals and states. My point here is that wherever we
find 'evidence' of the preference for transnational lifestyles
as compared to return, the situation should be examined
carefully. We should always ask which groups are being
encouraged to do what and by whom. Who prefers for
migrants or refugees to remain abroad and why? Are the

reasons primarily economical, or are they related to the home country's internal political power balance? What are the differences between refugees who are seen as potential troublemakers and/or economic burdens, whose state of origin prefers for them to stay abroad, and displaced people, who are vulnerable victims needing to return to their proper place as soon as possible through humanitarian interventions in the name of human security, whose goal is to protect people rather than state borders? In the case of Palestinian return migration to the West Bank and the Gaza Strip in the aftermath of the Gulf War of 1990–1991 and again shortly after the Oslo Accords of 1993, most returnees were not refugees because the Oslo Accords did not allow Palestinian refugees the right of return.

Conclusions

In terms of both Western entrance policies and development-oriented aid, refugees and asylum seekers are increasingly treated either as security threats or as economic migrants. The terms 'refugee' and 'economic migrant' are thus interpreted contextually. With regard to the European Union entrance policy, the association between the two terms points to potential system abuse. The mobility of refugees is being controlled, yet, simultaneously, refugees are expected to carry much of the responsibility for the post-conflict reconstruction of their home communities, through investments and remittances to the most vulnerable—those who stayed behind. Obviously, taking advantage of transnational connections and linking diaspora populations to post-conflict reconstruction often benefits all parties concerned. However, involving refugees and migrants in 'reconstruction' and development should not happen through guest worker types of migration regimes that are

currently re-emerging in the West. These exploitative systems are being legitimated as development tools and as a
solution to refugee problems by using security concerns to
restrict migrants' and refugees' freedom of movement and
their right to seek asylum.

The transnational approach, as applied to development
policies, has not taken over at the expense of the strategy
of combating the root causes of migration. Rather, the
promotion of transnational relations as a development
tool and as a lasting solution to the refugee crisis shows
signs of taking place within the framework of this strategy
through the links made between development and security. The politicization of transnationality seems to mean
that new security conceptualizations that emphasize
methodological individualism, whereby the individual is
the reference point of security, are increasingly operationalized on behalf of state security at the expense of refugee
and migrant security. Even if the new security understandings allegedly give up narrow state-centeredness, they
indicate the promotion of regionalism, in which refugee
crises are contained and solved in conflict regions. Thus,
while methodological individualism is a conceptual feature of human security, policies and practices that involve
refugees and migration reflect the concern of containing
refugees in conflict regions where transnational mobility would mainly be confined and secondary movement
strictly regulated. Consequently, despite conceptual over-
lapping with human rights, human security, at least on an
operational level, indicates particularism and relativism
when applied to refugees and migrants.

It is striking that migration scholars—specialists on the
motivations, considerations, hopes, and constraints that
refugees and migrants experience—have left the analysis of
the strategic relations of security and migration mainly to
security and political analysts, whose methodological and

theoretical tools are not necessarily as appropriate for the subject area. I suggest that migration researchers should go beyond analyzing how societal and security concerns of receiving states translate into state action against asylum seekers and migrants, and then trying to prove how well the migrants actually adapt and integrate. These scholars need to do much more than demonstrate how much migrants contribute to the development in both sending and host countries. Such approaches are understandable because many scholars who work with the transnational paradigm have adopted the migrants' perspective—subconsciously or explicitly—and are concerned about their rights and security. However, this has resulted in their accommodation to the politicized approach to transnationality without having addressed this politicization and its reasons analytically. Migration scholars should analyze securitization seriously and bring it to their scholarship without letting that trend guide their research through state policies. This indicates accepting neither methodological nationalism nor methodological individualism and addressing the global reach of a set of powerful states and related institutional structures. A scholarship is needed that examines refugees and migrants as subjects of security, not simply as indicators of a lack of security. Only then will it be possible to bring different units of analysis, such as states and international organizations, into a single analytical perspective.

Notes

1. On a macro-economic level, Orozco (2003) characterizes the development impact of migration by 'five Ts': transfers (of remittances and grants), transportation, tourism, telecommunication, and trade (cf. Levitt and Sørensen 2004).

2. The figure of 190,600,000 total international migrants is obtained from the Migration Policy Institute's Web site. See http://www. migrationinformation.org/DataHub/remittances/ World.pdf.

3. Examples of this viewpoint are many. See, for example, the International Organization for Migration's special edition titled *Reaping the Fruits of Migration and Development* (IOM 2007), in which articles organized along policy lines, such as 'migrant training', 'economic sustainability', 'remittances', 'labor migration', etc., approach migrants as agents of development mainly 'back home'. Several articles concern return migration (e.g., to Afghanistan) and refugee repatriation, phenomena that I will reflect on throughout this text.

4. It is important to note that neo-liberalism is not a homogeneous phenomenon, but it works differently in different contexts, also development and mobility.

5. 'Mobile livelihoods' is a term introduced by Karen Fog Olwig and Ninna Nyberg Sørensen (2002). It refers to making a living in a way that depends on multiple locations and border-crossing ties.

6. This, of course, does not suggest a break away from nationalism as an ideology. Scholars such as Wimmer and Glick Schiller (2002) who critique methodological nationalism do not advocate methodological individualism.

7. Individual terrorists of immigrant origin who do pose a threat to state security cannot be considered as representative of groups or categories such as refugees or migrants.

8. For the text of the European Commission's comments, see http:// ec.europa.eu/justice_home/news/intro/wai/news_040603_ en.htm (cf. Sørensen 2004).

9. EADS took part in the 2nd International Conference on European Emergency Management, "Civil Protection—Resilience to Terrorism and Natural Disasters," which was held in Helsinki on 12–14 November 2008. The event was organized by the CIVPRO Civil Protection Network, Aleksanteri Institute, University of Helsinki, and was sponsored by the prime minister's office of Finland, the US embassy in Helsinki, and the EU Commission. Other corporate partners included Elisa Corporation, Siemens, Hedman Partners, Jalasvirta Group, and Ourex.

10. 'Contractor states' and 'caretaker governments' also appear in post-conflict contexts. For example, since the mid-1990s, this approach toward aid implementation has been critiqued by Palestinian laypeople and academics who are concerned by the

relationships among the Palestinian National Authority, Israel, the United States, and the international donor community (see Isotalo 2009).

11. The ethnographic material about Palestinian return migrants that I discuss here was collected in the occupied Palestinian territory and Israel during more than two years of fieldwork between 1996 and 2003.

References

Annan, Kofi. 2005. *In Larger Freedom: Towards Development, Security and Human Rights for All.* http://www.un.org/largerfreedom/(accessed 27 August 2009).

Basch, Linda, Nina Glick Schiller, and Cristina Stanton Blanc. 1994. *Nations Unbound: Transnational Projects, Postcolonial Predicaments, and Deterritorialized Nation-States.* New York: Gordon and Breach.

Bourne, Ralph. 1916. "Trans-national America." *Atlantic Monthly* 118: 86–97.

Boutros-Ghali, Boutros. 1992. *An Agenda for Peace.* http://www.un.org/Docs/SG/agpeace.html (accessed 27 August 2009).

Brouwer, Evelien, Petra Catz, and Elspeth Guild, eds. 2003. *Immigration, Asylum and Terrorism: A Changing Dynamic in European Law.* Nijmegen: Instituut voor Rechtssociologie.

Ceccorulli, Michela. 2009. "Migration as a Security Threat: Internal and External Dynamics in the European Union." GARNET Working Paper No. 65, April.

Chimini, B. S. 2000. "Globalisation, Humanitarianism and the Erosion of Refugee Protection." RSC Working Paper No. 3. Oxford: Refugee Studies Centre, Oxford University.

Curle, Adam. 1971. *Making Peace.* London: Tavistock Publications.

Dezalay, Yves, and Bryant Garth. 2002. *Global Prescriptions: The Production, Exportation and Importation of a New Legal Orthodoxy.* Ann Arbor: University of Michigan Press.

Duffield, Michael. 2001. *Global Governance and the New Wars: The Merging of Development and Security.* London: Zed Books.

EUPOL (European Union Police). 2009. *TE-SAT 2009: EU Terrorism Situation and Trend Report.* http://www.europol.europa.eu/publications/EU_Terrorism_Situation_and_Trend_Report_TE-SAT/TESAT2009.pdf.

European Union. 2003. *A Secure Europe in a Better World: European Security Strategy*. http://www. consilium.europa.eu/uedocs/cmsUpload/78367.pdf (accessed 5 September 2008).

———. 2008. *Report on the Implementation of the European Security Strategy: Providing Security in a Changing World*. http://www.consilium.europa.eu/ueDocs/cms_Data/docs/pressData/en/reports/104630.pdf (accessed 10 June 2009).

Ferguson, James. 1997. "Anthropology and Its Evil Twin: 'Development' in the Constitution of a Discipline." Pp. 150–175 in *International Development and Social Sciences: Essays on the History and Politics of Knowledge*, ed. Frederick Cooper and Randall Packard. Berkeley: University of California Press.

Glick Schiller, Nina. 2003. "The Centrality of Ethnography in the Study of Transnational Migration: Seeing Wetland Instead of the Swamp." Pp. 99–128 in *American Arrivals: Anthropology Engages the New Immigration*, ed. Nancy Foner. Santa Fe, NM: School of American Research Press.

———. 2005. "Transnationality." Pp. 448–467 in *A Companion to the Anthropology of Politics*, ed. David Nugent and Joan Vincent. Malden, MA: Blackwell.

Goodwin-Gill, Guy. 1999. "Editorial: Refugees and Security." *International Journal of Refugee Law* 11, no. 1: 1–5.

Hammerstad, Anne. 2000. "Whose Security? UNHCR, Refugee Protection and State Security after the Cold War." *Security Dialogue* 31, no. 4: 391–403.

IOM (International Organization for Migration). 2007. *Migration: Reaping the Fruits of Migration and Development. A Special Edition*. July. http://publications.iom.int/bookstore/free/Migration_July%202007_EN.pdf.

Isotalo, Riina. 2009. "Gendered Palestinian Citizenship: Women, Legal Pluralism and Post-conflict Aid." Pp. 217–252 in *Women and War in the Middle East: Transnational Perspectives*, ed. Nadje Al-Ali and Nicola Pratt. London: Zed Books.

Kaldor, Mary. 2007. *Human Security: Reflections on Globalization and Intervention*. Cambridge: Polity Press.

Koser, Khaled, and Richard Black, eds. 1999. *The End of the Refugee Cycle? Refugee Repatriation and Reconstruction*. Oxford: Berghahn Books.

Levitt, Peggy, and Nina Glick Schiller. 2004. "Conceptualizing Simultaneity: A Transnational Social Field Perspective on Society." *International Migration Review* 38, no. 145: 595–629.

Levitt, Peggy, and Ninna Nyberg Sørensen. 2004. "The Transnational Turn in Migration Studies." *Global Migration Perspectives*, no. 6 (October). http://www.gcim.org/gmp/Global%20Migration%20Perspectives%20No%206.pdf.

Loescher, Gil. 1992. *Refugee Movements and International Security*. Oxford: Oxford University Press.

Loescher, Gil, and James Milner. 2005. *Protracted Refugee Situations: Domestic and International Security Implications*. London: Routledge.

Nye, Joseph S., Jr. 1976. "Independence and Interdependence." *Foreign Policy* 22: 130–161.

Ogata, Sadako. 1999. "Human Security: A Refugee Perspective." Keynote speech at the Ministerial Meeting on Human Security Issues of the "Lysoen Process" Group of Governments, Bergen, Norway, 19 May. http://www.unhcr.org/3ae68fc00.html.

Ogata, Sadako, and Amartya Sen. 2003. *Human Security Now: Commission on Human Security*. http://humansecurity-chs.org/finalreport/English/FinalReport.pdf (accessed 26 August 2009).

Olwig, Karen Fog, and Ninna Nyberg Sørensen. 2002. "Mobile Livelihoods: Making a Living in the World." Pp. 1–20 in *Work and Migration: Life and Livelihoods in a Globalizing World*, ed. Ninna Nyberg Sørensen and Karen Fog Olwig. London: Routledge.

Orozco, Manuel. 2003. "Remittances to Latin America: Money, Markets, and Costs." Paper presented at "Remittances as a Development Tool" conference, InterAmerican Development Bank, Washington, DC, 26 February.

Østergaard-Nielsen, Eva. 2003. *Transnational Politics: Turks and Kurds in Germany*. London: Routledge.

Owen, Taylor. 2008. "The Uncertain Future of Human Security in the UN." *International Social Science Journal* 59, no. s1: 113–127.

Pastore, Ferruccio. 2003. "'More Development for Less Migration' or 'Better Migration for More Development'? Shifting Priorities in the External Dimension of European Migration Policy." Paper presented at the Cicero Foundation International Seminar for Experts on European Migration and Refugee Policy, Rome 13–14 November.

Peltonen, Riikka. 2007. "By Patera to Fortress Europe: A Study of West African Migrants in the Canaries." MA thesis, University of Helsinki.

Piper, Nicola. 2006. "Gendering the Politics of Migration." *International Migration Review* 40, no. 1: 133–164.

Ratha, Dilip, Sanket Mohapatra, and Zhimei Xu. 2008. "Outlook for Remittance Flows 2008–2010: Growth Expected to Moderate Significantly, but Flows to Remain Resilient." *Migration and Development Brief 8*, November.

Rosen, David. 2007. "Child Soldiers, International Humanitarian Law, and the Globalization of Childhood." *American Anthropologist* 109, no. 2: 296–306.

Safran, William. 1991. "Diasporas in Modern Societies: Myths of Homeland and Return." *Diaspora* 1, no. 1: 83–99.

Slim, Hugo. 2001. "Violence and Humanitarianism: Moral Paradox and the Protection of Civilians." *Security Dialogue* 32, no. 3: 325–339.

Sørensen, Ninna Nyberg. 2004. "The Development Dimension of Migrant Transfers." DIIS Working Paper No. 2004/16. Copenhagen: Danish Institute for International Studies.

———. 2005. "Den Globale Familie—Oplösning Eller Transnationalisering af Familien?" *Dansk Sociologi* 1, no. 16: 71–89.

Sørensen, Ninna Nyberg, Nicholas Van Hear, and Poul Engberg-Pedersen. 2003. "The Migration-Development Nexus: State of the Art Overview." Pp. 5–50 in *The Migration-Development Nexus*, ed. Nicholas Van Hear and Ninna Nyberg Sørensen. Geneva: International Organization for Migration.

Stepputat, Finn. 2004. "Dynamics of Return and Sustainable Reintegration in a 'Mobile Livelihoods' Perspective." DIIS Working Paper No. 2004/10. Copenhagen: Danish Institute for International Studies.

Turner, Mandy. 2006. "Building Democracy in Palestine: Liberal Peace Theory and the Election of Hamas." *Democratization* 13, no. 5: 739–755.

UNHCR (United Nations High Commissioner for Refugees). 1995. *The State of the World's Refugees: In Search of Solutions.* Oxford: Oxford University Press.

———. 1996–1997. *UNHCR Strategy Towards 2000.* Geneva: UNHCR.

———. 1997. *State of the World's Refugees: A Humanitarian Agenda.* Geneva: UNHCR.

United Nations. 2005. *Report of the Trade and Development Board on Its Resumed Fifty-Second Session*, 7 November. http://www.unctad.org/en/docs/tdb52d10vol1a1_en.pdf (accessed 10 June 2009).

UNDP (United Nations Development Programme). 1993. *Human Development Report: People's Participation*. Oxford: Oxford University Press.

_____. 1994. *Human Development Report: New Dimensions of Human Security*. Oxford: Oxford University Press.

_____. 2009. *Human Development Report: Overcoming Barriers: Human Mobility and Development*. Oxford: Oxford University Press.

Van Hear, Nicholas. 1998. *New Diasporas: The Mass Exodus, Dispersal and Regrouping of Migrant Communities*. London: University College London Press.

_____. 2002. "From 'Durable Solutions' to 'Transnational Relations': Home and Exile among Refugee Diasporas." CDR Working Paper No. 02.9. July. Copenhagen: Centre for Development Research.

van Selm, Joanne, and Eleni Tsolakis. 2004. "The Enlargement of an 'Area of Freedom, Security and Justice': Managing Migration in a European Union of 25 Members." *Policy Brief*, Migration Policy Institute, May.

Wimmer, Andreas, and Nina Glick Schiller. 2002. "Methodological Nationalism and Beyond: Nation-State Building, Migration and the Social Sciences." *Global Networks* 2, no. 4: 301–334.

UNDERSTANDING THE RELATIONSHIP BETWEEN MIGRATION AND DEVELOPMENT

Toward a New Theoretical Approach

Raúl Delgado Wise and
Humberto Márquez Covarrubias

Led by the World Bank and the Inter-American Development Bank, some international organizations have been pursuing an international political agenda in the areas of migration and development. They posit that remittances sent home by migrants can promote local, regional, and national development in the countries of origin. By extension, remittances are seen as an indispensable source of foreign exchange that provides macro-economic stability and alleviates the ravages caused by insidious problems such as poverty. This view is supported by the growing importance of remittances as a source of foreign exchange and subsistence income for many households in underdeveloped countries. The United Nations Development Programme (UNDP 2007) has estimated that 500 million people (8 percent of the world's population) receive remittances. According to World Bank (2006) figures, remittances sent home by emigrants from underdeveloped countries rose from US $85 billion in 2000 to US $199 billion in 2006. If unrecorded flows through informal channels are considered, this figure may increase recorded flows by 50 percent or more (ibid.). Taking these unrecorded flows into account, the overall amount of remittances surpassed foreign direct investment flows and more than doubled official aid received by Third World countries. In many cases, remittances have become the largest and least volatile source of foreign exchange earnings.

Although the World Bank's position vis-à-vis the relationship between remittances and migration has recently become more cautious (Lapper 2006), it should be pointed out that the impact of the implementation of structural adjustment programs as a key element of the neo-liberal policy promoted by the World Bank and the International Monetary Fund (IMF) is the root cause of the upsurge in South-North migration and remittance flows. Moreover, far from contributing to the development of migrant-sending countries, structural adjustment programs have reinforced the dynamics of underdevelopment.

The great paradox of the migration-development agenda is that it leaves the principles that underpin neo-liberal globalization intact and does not affect the specific way in which neo-liberal policies are applied in migrant-sending countries (Castles and Delgado Wise 2008; Delgado Wise and Márquez Covarrubias 2007). At most, it offers superficial strategies involving migration, but it does not address issues of development, such as the need to lower the cost of transferring remittances or to promote financial support infrastructures that enable the use of remittances in micro-projects (which, ultimately, have very limited impact in terms of development). It is clear that the policies currently under design are neither coherent nor properly contextualized, and could not serve as part of an alternative development model or a new form of regional economic integration, which would be capable of reducing the socio-economic asymmetries that exist between sending and receiving countries. For that matter, they would also fail to contain—or at least reduce—the current and burgeoning migratory flows.

This essay underscores the need for a theoretical approach based on the political economy of development. From this perspective, special attention is placed on the role of migrant labor and remittances (which are chiefly assessed as a wage component) as part of a complex set of transnational social relations, used for the subsistence of a surplus population that is forced to enter cross-border job markets under conditions of labor precarization and social exclusion. In our attempt to cast light on the relationship between migration and development, we address a variety of theoretical approaches while searching for a comprehensive, multi-dimensional view.[1]

This essay is divided into three sections, the first of which offers a brief overview of current theoretical models for analyzing the migration-development relationship. The second section introduces our proposed analytical model based on the political economy of development. In the third and concluding section, we highlight some of the basic ideas underlying our alternative conceptualization of the relationship between development and migration.

The Relationship between Development and Migration: A Brief Theoretical Overview

Despite the boom in migration and development research, there is a clear dissociation between theories of development and theories of migration. This results in extremely restricted studies that do not capture the context within which migrations—and the fundamental connections involving processes of global, national, regional, or local development—are inscribed. It is important to point out that conceptual and theoretical research has been lagging behind the discourse and the migration and development policies promoted by international organizations. Consequently, academic debate has been largely limited to a conceptual reproduction of said discourse or, at best, to establishing a critical distance from it.

The theory and practice of development underwent a historical change after World War II, when the interests of hegemonic nations (mainly the United States) took precedence. During the 1950s and in the context of the Cold War, the concept of modernization was employed on behalf of an imperialist project. In Latin America, however, the asymmetrical relationship between development and underdevelopment was amply explored during this period (e.g., the structuralism of the Economic Commission for Latin America and the Caribbean, or the ECLAC, and theories of dependency). With the imposition of neo-liberalism toward the end of the 1970s and in the early 1980s, concerns about development became secondary, and alternative approaches were politically blocked as socio-economic dynamics became subject to market regulation. The emergence of this distinct discourse hampered theoretical reflection on development and its political practice, giving way to a genuine counter-revolution. Faced with the deepening asymmetries between developed and underdeveloped countries, the increase of social inequalities among national populaces, and a diversity of social conflicts, the promoters of neo-liberal globalization have resumed the discourse of development. Far from proposing structural and institutional changes, however, this just seeks to provide neo-liberalism with a 'human face'.

On the one hand, we have seen a series of attempts to reconceptualize development from an interdisciplinary perspective and, in cases such as community-based approaches, to reappraise the problems of underdeveloped nations. These assorted and incipient efforts are highly eclectic (Parpart and Veltmeyer 2004) and often end up being subsumed by the neo-liberal mold. On the other hand, even though there is a nominal consensus regarding the values and goals of development theories (e.g., social welfare, higher quality of life, participation, etc.), little attention has been given to the causes of underdevelopment and how to deal with them, with what resources, under whose leadership, and in what direction to produce social change. In other words, we still need to work on the structural and strategic production of an integral vision that addresses the root causes of the considerable asymmetries among countries and the social inequalities that dominate contemporary capitalism.

The most influential migration studies have been undertaken by research centers in developed countries (which, for obvious reasons, are the major immigrant receivers on the planet). These have failed to pay enough attention to the underdeveloped context of the migrant-sending countries, which is one of the reasons for such copious migratory flows. There is as yet no theoretical-conceptual framework that takes into account the point of view and particular interests of underdeveloped countries, which, at this point, are seasoned exporters of cheap workforces that are both qualified and unqualified. Generally speaking, the migratory issue has been analyzed from a decontextualized perspective, which tends toward an ethnocentric and individualistic stance that focuses on partial aspects responding to the rationale of methodological nationalism (e.g., salary disparities, the displacement of native workers, illegality, and border security). This vision not only distorts reality but also obscures the underlying causes of the problem and potential ways of engaging it;

neo-classical economy and nativistic and xenophobic sociological approaches are among some of its representatives. Nativism, in fact, has been a highly popular stance in the political debate of receiving countries.

At the same time, receiving countries have also been the source of the transnationalism theory, which posits that immigrants establish a series of social relations that are constant, permanent, and characterized by cooperation with and reciprocity toward those who remain in the places of origin. By providing a more comprehensive vision of the migratory phenomenon and describing the multiplicity of social practices established by migrants, this theory brings valuable contributions to migration studies. Yet its attempt to explain migration as part of a configuration of social networks spanning immigrants' integration into the receiving society and their relationships with their places of origin bypasses a careful analysis of the development issues and processes in a given context (see Glick Schiller, this volume, for a related critique). Additional types of research focus on the new destinies of Mexican migration and the recent forms of precarization and labor segmentation in a mainly descriptive manner.

In terms of theoretical diversity, the current studies on international migration have certainly been prolific, and they have also provided us with abundant empirical evidence. This is apparent when we compare contrasting paradigms such as historic-structural (primitive accumulation, overpopulation, world system) with neo-classical theoretical standpoints and other approaches such as 'push-pull' (which comprises various analytical perspectives), the new economy, the segmented labor market theory, the 'migration hump' (a neo-Malthusian approach associated with a re-emergence of modernization theories), and the diverse socio-cultural perspectives (social networks, accumulative causation, and transnationalism).[2] However, we can also see how, in most cases, the interpretive strength is hampered by the lack of strong theoretical constructs or by the use of partial or isolationist theories that address only limited aspects of the phenomenon. These also tend to focus on a given phase of the migratory process (origin, development, or consolidation), with few attempting to cover the ample range of migratory dynamics from a multi-dimensional and multi-spatial perspective and to inscribe it in the global and regional integration contexts in which it is embedded. Although there are growing attempts to integrate the micro, meso, and macro levels of this phenomenon, the Northern perspective (i.e., that belonging to the receiving nations) is still preponderant, and the emphasis on development is still marginal.

Most of the studies that address the relationship between migration and development tend to focus on the first factor, as if migration were an independent variable and development possibilities were subject to, and depended on, the resources and initiatives of migrants. Additionally, they tend to center on local, communitarian, or regional aspects and on the role played by remittances, providing little insight into issues of development and neglecting the crucial element of macro-structure (Delgado Wise and Márquez Covarrubias 2006). Generally speaking, these analytical approaches are split into two major and apparently clashing trends:

1. *The vicious circle.* Migration and development are approached as antithetical concepts, particularly in connection with South-North labor migration. Migration is considered incapable of inducing dynamics of development in places of origin; instead, it is associated with adverse effects, such as inflation, productive disarticulation, reduced economic activity, and depopulation, all of which in turn lead to more

emigration. These views, however, do not constitute a theoretical model of migration and development. Rather, they are diagnoses that describe, from different angles, a dominant historical trend in countries and regions with high levels of migration. This approach has been taken by researchers such as Delgado Wise (2000), Papadimetriou (1998), and many others.

2. *The virtuous circle.* Mature migratory processes with consolidated social networks and established migrant organizations are believed capable of assisting (albeit in a limited way) local and regional development. This viewpoint engages the limited amount of social development that is allowed by neo-liberal policies in migrant-sending countries and includes a broad range of authors and analytical perspectives (some of them clashing) that emphasize remittances and/or migrant organizations. At the forefront of this trend stand politically influential international agencies, such as the World Bank (2005) and the Inter-American Development Bank (IADB 2000), which are interested in promoting a post-Washington Consensus neo-liberal policy. Secondly, there are those authors who have developed an outlook that is closer to the interests of migrant society and, in an approach that could be called 'transnationalism from below', emphasizes the role of migrant organizations as potential subjects of regional and local development (García Zamora 2005; Guarnizo and Smith 1998; Moctezuma 2005). The theory of the migration hump can be included here, from a neo-Malthusian, modernist viewpoint.

These two analytical variants share one characteristic: they take a unidirectional approach to migration and development, even though one denies the existence of development possibilities, and the other considers this a plausible process. Since the second trend has gained far more notoriety, it is important to recount some of the major academic postulates that comprise it in order to assess its achievements and limitations.

Remittances and productive investment. During the last two decades of the twentieth century, the flow of Mexican workers to the United States increased notoriously with the implementation of neo-liberal policies and the productive restructuring of the US economy. Studies on migration and development (focusing on remittances, investment, and development) have undergone two successive periods that have fundamentally influenced an ongoing debate that has yet to provide theoretical or practical solutions to the problem. In the 1980s, Mines (1981), Reichert (1981), Stuart and Kearney (1981), and Wiest (1984) undertook several empirical studies in the central-west region of Mexico that addressed the role played by migrants' remittances and argued that these had a negative effect in communities of origin, leading to social differentiation, land price inflation, and the accumulation of local resources into the hands of a given few. Subsequently, researchers would posit that these results took a negative view of remittance-based regional development.

During the 1990s, the cycle between remittances and productive investment was analyzed (Durand 1994; Durand, Parrado, and Massey 1996; Jones 1995; Massey and Parrado 1998). The results indicated that remittances were invested on agricultural and human capital and that the circulating money had a beneficial multiplying effect in communitarian, municipal, and regional economies. Knowing that remittances provide families with subsistence funds and, to a lesser extent, constitute productive investments, some authors (Durand 1994; Jones 1995) have argued that these investments have a substantial impact on specific sectors and localities. Massey and Parrado (1998: 19) maintain that international migration is a "source of production capital and a dynamic force that promotes entrepreneurial activity, the founding of businesses and economic expansion." As far as the financing of productive investments and social infrastructure is concerned, collective remittances would have to be added to migrants' savings (Goldring 1996; Moctezuma 2000; Smith 1998), particularly in high-migration areas where public and private investment are negligible.

Overall, the most interesting aspect of this research is the identification of a new social subject, the 'collective migrant' (Moctezuma 1999). This viewpoint, however, has been classified as optimistic, just like the prevalent discourse of the 1980s has been characterized as pessimistic. Institutions such as the ECLAC (Torres 2001) and the World Bank (Ratha 2003) have also been criticized for painting an overly optimistic picture of the phenomenon. There is consensus regarding the fact that a substantial portion of remittances is destined to cover families' basic needs (food, dress, housing, even education and health), but none regarding the potential role of remittances as investment sources or capital. In addition, some have criticized migration and development studies that center on remittances (Binford 2002; Canales and Montiel 2004).

Transnationalism and development. Contrary to the assumption that migrants almost invariably cease contact with their place of origin once they have settled in their country of destination, transnationalism underscores quite the opposite: regardless of their incorporation into the receiving society, migrants tend to maintain strong ties with their society of origin (Basch, Glick Schiller, and Blanc 1994; Glick Schiller and Fouron 2001). Authors who support this view argue that (1) migrants maintain bonds to their place of origin in order to deal with racial inequality and other hurdles in the country of destination; (2) migration is caused by global processes that supersede the nation-state and generates a global civil society that threatens the political monopoly exercised by the state, and (3) transnationalism gives way to a 'third space' that locates migrants between the sending and receiving states and their origin and destination societies. A distinction is made between 'transnationalism from above', the environment where corporate, financial, and governmental agents move, and 'transnationalism from below', the common space occupied by migrants. This approach opens up the possibility of observing, to a degree, the relation between development and migratory processes. In the first case, the subjects of study would be transnational companies such as remittance transfer services, banks, and generally all businesses that provide merchandise and/or services to migrants and their families. In the second case, the focus would be on the role played by migrants and their families as consumers in their place of origin.

The associations between transnationalism and development have been explored from at least two viewpoints. The first looks at the economy of migration, where the transnational practices of migrants—such as telephone calls, the use of communications technologies, participation in tourism and the nostalgia industry, and remittances—have positive effects on local economies (Orozco 2003) but also create niches that are later appropriated by transnational corporations (Guarnizo 2003). The second analyzes the contribution of migrant organizations to local and regional development processes, particularly their participation in social works that collectively benefit local populations (Delgado Wise, Márquez Covarrubias, and Rodríguez Ramírez 2004; Faist 2005; Portes, Escobar, and Walton 2006).

Co-development. Some nations of the European Union (France and, more recently, Italy and Spain) have designed country-specific policies of co-development, which are based on migrants' potential development contributions to their places of origin with the support of the developed nations. Co-development seeks to (1) promote productive activities through remittances; (2) educate migrants and encourage their return to their places of origin; (3) involve migrants in cooperation projects; (4) educate and guide potential emigrants in places of origin; (5) promote the creation of bridges between communities of origin in the South and those who have emigrated to the North; (6) foster interaction between national governments, local civic and business organizations, universities, educational and cultural centers, and migrants; and (7) improve the living and working conditions of migrants. In practice, co-development has been used as a supra-governmental policy to control immigration flow, while less attention has been paid to the promotion of development in countries of migratory origin. The actors involved in the process of co-development (governments, migrant organizations, and NGOs) do not necessarily see eye to eye on a number of issues, since their interpretations of this concept are usually shaped by their particular interests. Additionally, co-development is, in actuality, a paradox: less-developed European Union countries such as Spain received support to increase their national development to the extent that they went from being emigrant senders to immigrant receivers (Agrela and Dietz 2005). But when it comes to the outside, and despite the ongoing demand for cheap, imported workers, the European Union has created a sort of fortress (Bendel 2005) that seems to close its doors on immigration, using co-development to cover up immigration regulation policies involving countries that lie beyond its borders rather than actively pursuing development in these nations.

Migrant social subjects and local development. In the particular case of Mexico, Moctezuma (2005) has observed different types of migrants (collective, enterprising, savings-focused, and retired) and the roles that they play in terms of social and productive investments. García Zamora (2005) has proposed the establishment of a fund for local development and the adoption of a micro-financing system, while Delgado Wise and Rodríguez Ramírez (2001) have suggested that migrant organizations could promote regional development projects coupled with public policies. From our perspective, the implementation of development alternatives in local and regional spaces can be seen as a political problem that demands the construction of a new, collective social subject—one that involves migrant and non-migrant sectors and that channels the state's participation in a scheme of participative planning. This, however, requires the creation of public policies that generate spaces where remittance investments can have a significant, multiplying impact on the macro-economic level. The failure to accomplish this will result in limited migrant contributions.

In short, the field of migration and development studies has yet to establish firm bases and clearly defined boundaries. How, then, should we approach it? First of all, we can conclude that, regardless of existing theoretical weaknesses, there is a pragmatic and crucial link between international migration and development. Secondly, proponents of neo-liberal globalization are attempting to utilize migrants as a cosmetic concealment of—and the solution to—some of the more severe problems brought about by the very policies that this model promotes and seeks to entrench, both regionally and nationally. Thirdly, a vast amount of work currently falls into this field of studies, which is not well delimited. The relationship between migration and development lacks a proper theoretical background, and the theories of migration and development are deficient in themselves. There is also a proliferation of incomplete and disjointed studies that tend to be of a descriptive nature and lack a proper contextualization of the neo-liberal, globalized framework in which the migratory phenomenon takes place.

The Political Economy of Migration and Development: Toward a New Theoretical Approach

Despite the current popularity of migration-development studies, the analytical complexity of this subject requires an alternative approach that does not center on the migratory phenomenon but rather focuses on the other side of the equation—that is, on the macro-processes of development (see fig. 1). This new analytical perspective views migration as an aspect of the problems surrounding development and approaches development as a field of structural dynamics and strategic practices that take place on global, regional, national, and local levels. The predominantly theoretical and political approach taken by developed, migrant-receiving countries has created a hegemonic vision that must be transcended and complemented in order to incorporate the viewpoints of the underdeveloped, sending countries. Given the predominance of nationalist or local-based approaches, it is also

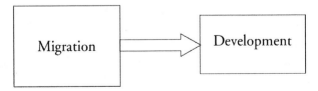

FIGURE 1 The Unidirectional Approach to the Migration-Development Relation

important to promote international comparative analyses that examine the interactions between processes of migration and development and the particular experiences taking place within them in the context of global capitalism.

We are of the opinion that the problem of international migration should be systematically incorporated in the field of development studies and that processes of under-development/development should be seen as a source of international migration (see fig. 2). In order to achieve this, we must shape theoretical objectives through inter-disciplinary exercise, that is, we need to formulate out-lines and propositions based on the context, agents, and processes of a multi-spatial environment. Additionally, it is necessary to problematize and contextualize the notion

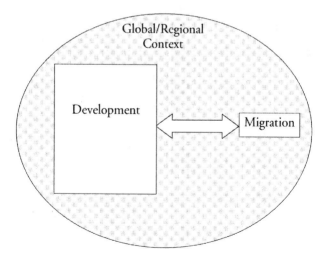

FIGURE 2 An Alternative Approach to the Migration-Development Interrelation

of development in order to break through normative frameworks that, failing to consider the need for structural and institutional change, limit the formulation of any socio-economic improvement to abstract terms. Moreover, in a context of large migration flows, the problem of development involves additional challenges such as the asymmetric relations between countries, the reconfiguration of productive chains, and the concomitant restructuring and precarization of the labor markets, trans-territorial social inequalities, and, more specifically, the decline of the material and subjective foundations that propitiates a given population's emigration, along with issues involving migrants' integration into receiving societies and their preservation of transnational ties.

From a theoretical and conceptual point of view, the initial challenge for researchers examining these issues is the lack of appropriate theoretical background. Also, the topic of migration has not been properly incorporated into the field of development studies. Having acknowledged the vast amount of academic work done in relation to these topics, we think that, in order to create a more integral approach to migration-development interrelations and to establish a concise theoretical and practical link between these two subjects, we must come up with a comprehensive analytical framework that includes aspects of socio-economic regional integration and looks at the development challenges faced by the sending countries.

This critical reconstruction also means that we should transcend the partial views of the phenomenon that have emerged from an agenda mainly centered on developed, migrant-receiving countries and that involve issues such as immigration regulation, national security, co-development, and the criminalization of migrants. It is crucial that we incorporate the experiences of underdeveloped, migrant-sending countries and view them in the context of contemporary capitalist development and the asymmetrical relationships between sending and receiving nations. The task of theorizing from an underdeveloped perspective, which implies a comprehensive view of capitalist asymmetries, is not new. From the 1950s to the 1970s, the ECLAC's theories of structuralism and Marxist-derived theories of dependency provided a solid basis in this regard (Bambirra 1978; Cardoso and Faletto 1969; Dos Santos 1974; Frank 1969; Furtado 1969; Marini 1973). Decades before the rise of transnationalist theories, these studies had already gone beyond the framework of methodological nationalism. Generally speaking, analysts from developed countries have displayed striking ignorance of (or disregard toward) theoretical contributions made by analysts from underdeveloped nations.

An analytical approach based on the political economy of development should allow us to transcend previously mentioned limitations and examine the following: (1) the wide range of interactions in the North-South (or development-underdevelopment) dynamic without losing sight of the differences intrinsic to each region; (2) the interaction between different spatial levels (local, national, regional, global) and social dimensions (economic, political, cultural, environmental); (3) ways of creating an interdisciplinary, critical model that aids in the reconstruction of reality as well as theoretical reflection, challenging the preponderant 'economistic' and 'structuralist' views; and (4) a notion of development that surpasses the limitations of normative and decontextualized concepts and takes into account the necessary role of social transformation (i.e., structural, strategic, and institutional changes) in the improvement of living conditions among the general population. This process of transformation must involve a range of actors, movements, agents, and social institutions operating on a variety of levels and planes.

Within the framework of the political economy of development and in the current context of neo-liberal globalization, the relationship between international migration and development involves a dialectical interaction that surpasses the preponderant unidirectional view of migration-development. In the specific case of South-North (or underdeveloped-developed) migration, we can point out the following links between them.

Underdevelopment constitutes a catalyst for forced migration to developed countries. In the context of neo-liberal globalization, developed countries employ an imperialist strategy of economic restructuring that internationalizes productive, commercial, and financial processes at the same time that it allows the countries in question to appropriate the natural resources, economic surplus, and cheap workforce of underdeveloped nations. The relationships maintained between industrialized countries and peripheral and post-colonial nations exacerbate the latter's conditions of underdevelopment. Underdeveloped countries find themselves with redundant population reserves (and, therefore, surplus population), while their members are unable to find working conditions that ensure their personal and family reproduction. This is the direct result of reduced accumulation processes derived from asymmetrical relations with developed nations (an unequal exchange that translates into diverse forms of surplus transference). These conditions are not socially sustainable and lead to forced migration, which we understand as population movements brought about by the lack of proper living and working conditions or life-threatening political or social conflicts. Forced migration can result in substantial population loss for countries of origin, sometimes even leading to relative or absolute depopulation. The loss of qualified and unqualified workers is also associated with the neglect of productive activities and the loss of potential wealth.

Migrants contribute to the receiving country's development. Industrialized nations demand large quantities of qualified and unqualified workers. In some cases, this human merchandise is rendered increasingly vulnerable and additionally devalued by the lack of required documentation. Firstly, this ongoing demand results from developed nations' increased accumulation capacity, which is derived from the transference of resources and surpluses from underdeveloped countries. Secondly, it is the consequence of processes of demographic transition and an aging population. Immigrants contribute to an overall cheapening of the workforce since they tend to be employed in work-intensive areas of production where they rescue or substitute a national workforce that tends to earn higher salaries and benefits. Although the qualified immigrant workforce belongs to an elite sector, it is still comparatively cheap, since an immigrant's salary is lower than that of a national citizen employed in the same position. In the case of both qualified and unqualified migrants, the receiving country reaps substantial benefits, having invested nothing in the formation of the human capital it now enjoys. Not only do immigrants provide static comparative advantages derived from a reduction in production costs, they also bring comparative dynamic benefits through their participation in accelerated innovation processes. Overall, working immigrants and their families internally strengthen the receiving country's market through consumption. Even the so-called nostalgia market entails the creation of consumer demand, which fortifies internal economic activity. Although immigrants' taxable contributions enrich the country's fiscal fund, they do not translate into the kinds of social benefits enjoyed by the national population, thus denoting a criterion of social exclusion. Immigrant workers also help pay for the current crisis faced by pension systems due to the massive retirement of the Baby Boomer generation. While these contributions counteract some of the effects brought about by the dismantling of the welfare state, they obviously do not constitute a long-term solution.[3]

Migrants help maintain precarious socio-economic stability in their countries of origin. Migrants' salary-based remittances contribute to the subsistence of family members in the country of origin.[4] To a lesser extent, remittances also help finance small businesses in a subsistence economy. The participative remittances collected by migrant organizations finance public works and social projects in the places of origin. In some cases, this practice has become institutionalized: the Mexican federal government's Tres-Por-Uno (3x1) program has been replicated in other countries. Migrants with savings or entrepreneurial plans use their money to finance micro-projects in their places of origin. The most important type of remittance is, however, the salary-based one that is intended for family subsistence, which means that the resources sent by migrants are rarely destined for processes of development and social transformation. In a macro-economic context, remittance sums serve neo-liberal governments that, not bothering to come up with actual development alternatives, use them as a currency source that sustains a fragile macro-economic stability. In some cases, remittances have even been used as a guarantee when incurring foreign debt. In the absence of any kind of alternative project, migrants are now portrayed as the 'heroes of development', an utterly cynical move that renders them responsible for the promotion of said development, while the state, opting for the conservative stance of minimal participation, is no longer held accountable. The strategy of market regulation postulated by fundamentalist neo-liberals lacks any sort of development plan that involves migrants, as well as other social sectors, and promotes processes of social transformation. In truth, underdeveloped countries fulfill a particular role as workforce reserves, and their potential development is obstructed by increasingly reduced national elites, who are subordinated to the interests of governing circles in developed countries and, to a great extent, the interests of US capital.

The promotion of development as social transformation could contain forced migration. Globalization theory depicts migration as inevitable; however, we must endorse, both in theory and in practice, the viability of alternative processes of development and do so on different levels. We must first redefine the asymmetrical terms that developed countries, aided by principles that have by now turned into fetishes (e.g., democracy, liberty, free trade), use to dominate underdeveloped ones. This involves the exposure of imperialist practices, which have created oceans of inequality and condemned vast regions of the world to marginalization, poverty, social exclusion, and uncontrolled migration. Those neo-liberal governments in underdeveloped countries that argue that migration is an inevitable process and, for the present, capitalize triumphantly on the benefits of remittances are operating under a logic that will inevitably collapse. A genuine process of social transformation involving the migrant and non-migrant sectors of society would seek not only to contain the overwhelming flow of forced migration but also to reverse the ongoing processes of social degradation that characterize underdevelopment and even pose a threat to human existence (Bello 2006; Harvey 2007).

Having taken all of the above into account, an approach based on the political economy of development would posit that international migration is the result of problems in the development process and that the migratory phenomenon has to be examined in this context in order reveal its root causes and effects. In order to study migration, its cause-and-effect interrelation with development, and the different stages that are integral to this dialectical interaction, we must take into account two fundamental analytical dimensions: strategic practices and structural dynamics (see fig. 3).

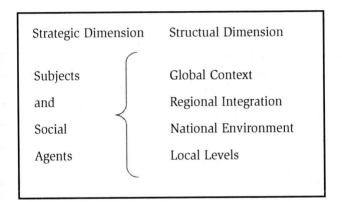

FIGURE 3 Analytical Dimensions of the Political Economy of Development

Strategic Practices

Strategic practices refer to the clashes between the diverging agendas that constitute the structural complex of contemporary capitalism and its inherent problems of development. Generally speaking, there are two major projects, which we call the 'hegemonic' and the 'alternative'. The hegemonic project is promoted by powerful transnational corporations in conjunction with the governments of developed countries, which are led by the United States, and allied to the power elites of some underdeveloped nations, as well as certain international organizations. Because the neo-liberal venture has lost legitimacy in recent years, rather than speak of hegemony we should speak of domination: more often than not, these policies are being implemented through military action and imposition rather than consensus. The alternative project comprises the socio-political actions taken by social movements and classes, as well as collective agents and subjects, in support of a political scheme designed to change the structural, political, and institutional dynamics that impede the implementation of alternative development policies on all levels (global, regional, national, and local).

The capacity to regulate development and migration is mostly in the hands of transnational corporations, developed migrant-receiving nations, and international organizations and their associated capital, the influence of which spans from the global to the local. The governments of underdeveloped, migrant-sending countries tend to lack a concise national project, are subordinated to the interests of powerful groups, and have limited influence in their own national and local milieus. Nevertheless, the dynamism and maturity acquired by some national diasporas (e.g., the Mexican diaspora) give way to new kinds of social subjects. This is particularly true in the case of migrant organizations, many of which promote development in their places of origin. Their actions are transnational in character, and although their involvement is not as intense in the countries of origin as it is in the countries of destination, their incipient participation in local development is noteworthy. Migrants, whether organized or not, maintain permanent and dynamic bonds with their places of origin and contribute (especially when organized) to the local processes taking place in the marginal spaces produced by the new world order. Subjects of migration have their own sphere of influence, and while some act across different levels, others are confined by their own niche and do not greatly influence the performance or interests of other actors.

Structural Dynamics

Structural dynamics refers to the asymmetrical ways in which contemporary capitalism is articulated. It includes the spheres of finance, commerce, production, and the labor market, as well as technological innovation (a strategic tool for the control of the aforementioned spheres), the use and allocation of natural resources, and the environmental impact of those materials. These structural demarcations shape the relationships between (1) developed countries, (2) developed and underdeveloped countries, and (3) underdeveloped countries. They also determine the spaces in which the diverse social sectors, groups, movements, and classes relate to each other. All of this is expressed differently, depending on whether it takes place on a global, regional, national, or local level.

Global context. Developed nations are currently immersed in a wide and complex process of capitalist restructuring that is taking place on a global scale. In addition to ongoing strategies such as information technology and communications innovations, economic tertiarization, and the internationalization of finance, the current major global strategies include the internationalization of production and the transnationalization, differentiation, and precarization of labor markets. In this sense, contemporary capitalism has created a new world order structured around neo-liberal globalization—a system that reproduces the economic asymmetries between developed and underdeveloped countries on an unprecedented scale at the same time that it deepens social inequalities, poverty, and marginalization on a global scale. The welfare state is being dismantled in both migrant-receiving and migrant-sending countries, while the flexibilization and precarization of the labor market increases and the environment irreversibly deteriorates. In this context, and despite its presence in the discourse of international organizations and governments, development has been abandoned and its goals eschewed. This is why, now more than ever, the pending issue of development is one of the major challenges facing contemporary humankind.

Regional integration. Developed countries now comprise regional economic blocs that, among other things, seek to expand territorially their internal markets, increase their production platform, and guarantee supplies of cheap labor, natural resources, and economic surplus. This is the case, for example, of the North American bloc and the European Union. Transnational labor markets are based on the availability of a cheap workforce and its impact on the ongoing productive restructuring (a sequel to the international capitalist crisis of the 1970s) that seeks to reduce production costs as a competitive strategy. For those underdeveloped countries that participate, directly or indirectly, in the scheme of regional integration led by the great capitalist powers, the exportation of a cheap workforce results in their increased international dependency. The configuration of a regional bloc involves a series of strategic articulations that include the transnationalization of financial markets and the restructuring and internationalization of production, among other processes. It additionally fosters the permanent cheapening and precarization of the workforce as a competitive weapon against other regional blocs, with the purpose of furthering production restructuring and increasing profit margins. The economy of cheap labor has been taken to unforeseeable extremes in the past few decades. It now lies at the heart of global capitalism and illustrates the way in which the immigrant workforce has gained access to developed nations: international labor migration has grown exponentially and, in doing so, has become a crucial piece in the new global mechanism.

Migrants' contributions now affect, to varying degrees, the economic, social, and cultural development of both sending and receiving countries. Still, many receiving countries exploit immigrants, subject them to xenophobia and racism, and blame them for a wide variety of social problems to the extent that they are considered criminals and their human, labor, social, and political rights are whisked away. When an underdeveloped nation inside a regional economic bloc becomes the source of substantial migratory flow toward a central country, this creates strong dependency ties that threaten labor sovereignty at the same time that they consolidate a specific migratory system. This does not mean that the core nation will come to depend on the cheap workforce of the sending country, since many other regions can supply laborers. In the specific case of the North American bloc, Mexico's relationship to the United States is conditioned by an asymmetrical pattern of subordination. Socio-economic asymmetries stem from the widely divergent structural situations in the two countries, and while the Unites States is the world's major capitalist power, Mexico is a dependent party that subordinates its political agenda and geo-strategic decisions to the interests of its northern neighbor. These processes of regional integration are not exclusive to trans-hemispheric North-South interactions. They also take place among countries in either hemisphere and have resulted in a certain reconfiguration of migratory flow, as countries of emigration simultaneously become countries of transit and immigration, and as South-North and South-South migration chains become established.

National environment. The neo-liberal policy of structural adjustment brings about a cycle of economic depression in underdeveloped economies, constrains the internal market, weakens the labor market, and encourages emigration toward developed nations. The emigrating workforce, which in its home country appears as broadly based over-population, is ultimately a working reserve at the service of productive, restructuring processes that are commanded by transnational corporations and Northern countries. The latter comprises, on the one hand, the destruction of productive chains and social production relations and, on the other, the construction of new bonds between developed and underdeveloped countries that exacerbate the dependency and exploitation of underdeveloped nations in both regional and global contexts. This policy also involves the dismantling of a development model (or a model of import substitution, in the case of Latin America) that included the presence of a welfare state and the introduction of a new social policy that does little more than channel meager resources to the most vulnerable sectors of society in an attempt to paint a human face on the social disaster brought about by neo-liberalism. During the 1980s, the Washington Consensus implemented neo-liberal policies of structural adjustment, including commercial and financial liberalization and institutional privatization. Recently, international organizations involved in the post–Washington Consensus era sought to humanize their choice of policies by raising subjects such as the fight against poverty, the promotion of equality, and social inclusion. The United Nations' development goals for the millennium take the same stance, but bypass any structural or institutional changes.

Local levels. Migrant-sending localities have become dependent on remittances that enable consumption and ensure family and social subsistence. Remittances are also expected to promote local development, and sending countries tend to perceive migrants, both socially and institutionally, as the pillar upon which the precarious macro-economic, political, and social situations of the nation rest. As if this were not enough, both sending countries and international organizations think of remittances as a purportedly strategic resource that will propitiate development—either nationally, regionally, or locally—and therefore will not commit to providing sufficient resources to propel actual development. In fact, remittances supplement the negligible public funds assigned to social development under neo-liberal decentralization programs. Finally, it is at the local level that socio-economic spaces are reconfigured and internal and international migration patterns are traced.

Final Thoughts

The theoretical framework proposed in this essay focuses on the following four aspects, which we consider to be fundamental for understanding the relationship between development and migration.

1. *A critical approach to neo-liberal globalization.* Counter to discourses that advocate its inevitability, we posit that the current phase of capitalism is unsustainable and illegitimate, and our present world order should and will undergo substantial changes.

2. *A critical reconstitution of the field of development studies.* The predominance of a singular mode of analysis that stressed the belief that the free market would work as a powerful regulatory mechanism, efficiently assigning resources and providing patterns of economic convergence among countries and their populations, has summarily failed. There is a need for new theoretical and practical alternatives, and we propose a revaluation of development as a process of social transformation through a multi-dimensional,

multi-spatial, and properly contextualized approach. This integral approach requires the inclusion of the viewpoints of the underdeveloped societies and the consideration of strategic and structural aspects, which should be examined at the global, regional, national, and local levels.

3. *The construction of an agent of change.* The globalizing project led by the United States has ceased to be consensual: it has benefited only capitalist elites and has excluded and damaged an overwhelming amount of people throughout the world. Economic, political, social, cultural, and environmental changes are all needed, but a transformation of this magnitude is not viable unless diverse movements, classes, and agents can establish common goals. The construction of an agent of change requires not only an alternative theory of development but also open dialogue: the sharing of experiences, the conciliation of interests and visions, and the construction of alliances in the framework of South-South and South-North relations.

4. *A reassessment of migration and development studies.* The current explosion of forced migration is part of the intricate machinery of neo-liberal globalization. In order to understand this process, we need to redefine the boundaries of studies that address migration and development. We need to expand our field of research and invert the terms of the present migration-development equation in order to situate the complex issues of development and underdevelopment at the center of the frame. This entails a new way of understanding international migration. Migrants should not be held responsible for the promotion of development in their places of origin. At the same time, it is important to highlight their direct contributions to the development of receiving

countries and their impact in their places of origin. It is fundamental to identify viable pathways to new stages of development where migration can be voluntary instead of forced, and this requires new theoretical and methodological approaches that result in the creation of new research agendas, concepts, analytical categories, and information systems. This last issue is an invitation to engage in constructive debate and the creation of new forms of collective, interdisciplinary, inter-institutional, and international research.

Notes

1. It should be pointed out that most studies regarding international migration reflect the concerns of those countries that receive migrants, that is, assimilation/integration, security, wage differentials, etc. In countries of origin, most studies involve demographic dynamics, remittance flows, ethnography, cultural impact, and related topics. In turn, development studies do not seriously address the problem of migration except as some form of secondary or external factor. In contrast, most of the studies addressing relations between migration and development have focused on the local, community, or regional aspects, overemphasizing the role of remittances, offering a limited view of development, and neglecting the transnational nature of the phenomenon and, more importantly, the macro-social variables that shape the migratory system (Delgado Wise and Márquez Covarrubias 2006).

2. In a recent study, Hein de Haas (2007) undertook a review of migration and development literature. The author questions the limited and equivocal manner in which some of the field's most respected researchers have described and classified the major theories on migration, particularly the 'economy of migration' and 'accumulative causation'.

3. The advance and development of migratory dynamics have created a complex social transnational space that engages societies of origin and destination and serves as a dynamic field of economic

activity. Economic opportunities in this field are usually seized by large corporations of developed countries (Guarnizo 2003).

4. For the different types of remittances, see Márquez Covarrubias (2006).

References

Agrela, Belén, and Gunther Dietz. 2005. "Emergencia de regimenes multinivel y diversificación público-privada de la política de inmigración en España." *Migración y Desarrollo* 4: 20–41.

Bambirra, Vania. 1978. *Teoría de la Dependencia: Una Anticrítica*. Mexico City: Ediciones Era.

Basch, Linda, Nina Glick Schiller, and Cristina Szanton Blanc. 1994. *Nations Unbound: Transnational Projects, Postcolonial Predicaments, and Deterritorialized Nation-States*. New York: Gordon and Breach.

Bello, Walden. 2006. "The Capitalist Conjuncture: Over-Accumulation, Financial Crises, and the Threat from Globalisation." *Third World Quarterly* 27, no. 8: 1345–1367.

Bendel, Petra. 2005. "¿Blindando la 'fortaleza europea'? Intereses, valores y cambios jurídicos en la política migratoria de la Unión Europea." *Migración y Desarrollo* 4: 54–65.

Binford, Leigh. 2002. "Remesas y subdesarrollo en México." *Relaciones* 23, no. 90: 115–158.

Canales, Alejandro, and Israel Montiel. 2004. "Remesas e inversión productiva en comunidades de alta migración a Estados Unidos: El caso de Teocaltiche, Jalisco." *Migraciones Internacionales* 2, no. 3: 142–172.

Cardoso, Fernando H., and Enzo Faletto. 1969. *Dependencia y desarrollo en America Latina*. Mexico City: Siglo XXI.

Castles, Stephen, and Raúl Delgado Wise, eds. 2008. *Migration and Development: Perspectives from the South*. Geneva: International Organization for Migration (IOM).

de Haas, Hein. 2007. "Migration and Development: A Theoretical Perspective." Paper presented at "Transnationalization and Development(s): Towards a North-South Perspective," Zentrum für interdisziplinäre Forschung, Bielefeld University, 31 May–1 June.

Delgado Wise, Raúl. 2000. "Consideraciones sobre la estructura económica y social de Zacatecas de cara al siglo XXI." Pp. 21–43 in *Los retos demográficos de Zacatecas en el siglo XXI*, ed. R. García Zamora and J. M. Padilla. Mexico City: UAZ.

Delgado Wise, Raúl, and Humberto Márquez Covarrubias. 2006. "The Mexico-United States Migratory System: Dilemmas of Regional Integration, Development, and Emigration." Paper presented at "Migration and Development: Perspectives from the South" conference, Bellagio, Italy, 10–13 July.

———. 2007. "The Reshaping of Mexican Labor Exports under NAFTA: Paradoxes and Challenges." *International Migration Review* 41, no. 3: 656–679.

Delgado Wise, Raúl, Humberto Márquez Covarrubias, and Héctor Rodríguez Ramírez. 2004. "Organizaciones transnacionales de migrantes y desarrollo regional en Zacatecas." *Migraciones Internacionales* 2, no. 4: 159–181.

Delgado Wise, Raúl, and Héctor Rodríguez Ramírez. 2001. "The Emergence of Collective Migrants and Their Role in Mexico's Local and Regional Development." *Canadian Journal of Development Studies* 22, no. 3: 1–18.

Dos Santos, Theotonio. 1974. *Dependencia y cambio social*. Buenos Aires: Amorrortu.

Durand, Jorge. 1994. *Más allá de la línea: Patrones migratorios entre México y Estados Unidos*. Mexico City: CNCA.

Durand, Jorge, Emilio A. Parrado, and Douglas S. Massey. 1996. "Migradollars and Development: A Reconsideration of the Mexican Case." *International Migration Review* 30, no. 2: 423–444.

Faist, Thomas. 2005. "Espacio social transnacional y desarrollo: Una exploración de la relación entre comunidad, Estado y mercado." *Migración y Desarrollo* 5: 2–34.

Frank, André Gunder. 1969. *Capitalismo y subdesarrollo en América Latina*. Buenos Aires: Siglo XXI.

Furtado, Celso. 1969. *Desarrollo y subdesarrollo*. Buenos Aires: Editorial Universitaria.

García Zamora, Rodolfo. 2005. "Migración, remesas y desarrollo: Los retos de las organizaciones migrantes mexicanas en Estados Unidos." PhD diss., Autonomous University of Zacatecas.

Glick Schiller, Nina, and Georges Fouron. 2001. *George Woke Up Laughing: Long-Distance Nationalism and the Search for Home*. Durham, NC: Duke University Press.

Goldring, Luin. 1996. "Blurring Borders: Constructing Transnational Community in the Process of Mexico-U.S. Migration." *Research in Community Sociology* 1: 69–104.

Guarnizo, Luis. 2003. "The Economics of Transnational Living." *International Migration Review* 37, no. 3: 666–699.

Guarnizo, Luis, and Michael Smith, eds. 1998. *Transnationalism from Below: Comparative Urban and Community Research.* New Brunswick, NJ: Transaction Publishers.

Harvey, David. 2007. "Neoliberalism as Creative Destruction." *Annals of the American Academy of Political and Social Science* 610, no. 1: 21–44.

IADB (Inter-American Development Bank). 2000. "Capitalización de remesas para desarrollo económico local." Donors memorandum.

Jones, Richard. 1995. *Ambivalent Journey: U.S. Migration and Economic Mobility in North-Central Mexico.* Tucson: University of Arizona Press.

Lapper, Richard. 2006. "Call for Caution Over by Migrants' Cash." *Financial Times*, 30 October. http://www.ft.com/cms/s/acc86cea-6839-11db-90ac-0000779e2340 (accessed 3 November 2006).

Marini, Ruy Mauro. 1973. *Dialéctica de la dependencia.* Mexico City: Ediciones Era.

Márquez Covarrubias, Humberto. 2006. "El desarrollo participativo transnacional basado en las organizaciones de migrantes." *Problemas del Desarrollo* 37, no. 144: 121–144.

Massey, Douglas, and Emilio Parrado. 1998. "International Migration and Business Formation in Mexico." *Social Science Quarterly* 1, no. 79: 1–34.

Mines, Richard. 1981. *Developing a Community Tradition of Migration to the United States: A Field Study in Rural Zacatecas, Mexico, and California Settlement Areas.* Monographs in U.S.-Mexican Studies No. 3. La Jolla, CA: Program in U.S.-Mexican Studies, University of California, San Diego.

Moctezuma, Miguel. 1999. "Redes sociales, comundaes filiales, familias y clubes de migrantes: El circuito migrante Sain Alto, Zac.-Oakland, Ca." PhD diss., El Colegio de la Frontera Norte, Tijuana.

———. 2000. "La organización de los migrantes zacatecanos en Estados Unidos." *Cuadernos Agrarios* 19–20: 81–104.

———. 2005. "Morfología y desarrollo de las asociaciones de migrantes mexicanos en Estados Unidos: Un sujeto social y político extraterritorial." *Migración y Desarrollo* 5: 59–85.

Orozco, Manuel. 2003. *Worker Remittances in an International Scope.* Washington, DC: Inter-American Dialogue.

Papadimetriou, Demetriou. 1998. "Reflections on the Relationship between Migration and Development." Paper presented at the

"International Migration and Development in North and Central America" seminar, Mexico City, 21–22 May.

Parpart, Jane, and Henry Veltmeyer. 2004. "The Development Project in Theory: A Review of Its Shifting Dynamics." Special Issue, *Canadian Journal of Development* 1: 39–60.

Portes, Alejandro, Cristina Escobar, and Alexandria Walton. 2006. "Organizaciones transnacionales de inmigrantes y desarrollo: Un estudio comparativo." *Migración y Desarrollo* 6: 3–44.

Ratha, Dilip. 2003. "Workers' Remittances: An Important and Stable Source of External Development Finance." Pp. 157–175 in World Bank, *Global Development Finance 2003: Striving for Stability in Development Finance.* Washington, DC: World Bank.

Reichert, Josua. 1981. "The Migration Syndrome: Seasonal U.S. Wage Labor and Rural Development in Central Mexico." *Human Organization* 1, no. 40: 56–66.

Smith, Robert. 1998. "Transnational Localities: Community Technology and the Politics of Membership within the Context of Mexico and U.S. Migration." *Comparative Urban and Community Research* 6: 196–238.

Stuart, James, and Michael Kearney. 1981. "Causes and Effects of Agricultural Labor Migration from the Mixteca of Oaxaca to California." Working Paper in U.S.-Mexican Studies No. 28: 11–15. La Jolla, CA: Program in U.S.-Mexican Studies, University of California, San Diego.

Torres, Federico. 2001. "Uso productivo de las remesas en México, Centroamérica y la República Dominicana: Experiencias recientes." Paper presented at the Conference on Migration in the Americas, Economic Commission for Latin America, San José, 4–6 September.

UNDP (United Nations Development Programme). 2007. *Human Development Report 2007: Human Development and Climate Change.* New York: United Nations Development Programme.

Wiest, Raymond. 1984. "External Dependency and the Perpetuation of Temporary Migration to the United States." Pp. 110–135 in *Patterns of Undocumented Migration: Mexico and the United States,* ed. Richard C. Jones. Totowa, NJ: Rowman & Allanheld.

World Bank. 2005. *Perspectivas para la Economía Mundial 2006.* Washington, DC: World Bank.

_____. 2006. *Global Economic Prospects 2006: Economic Implications of Remittances and Migration.* Washington: World Bank.

ADVERSARY ANALYSIS AND THE QUEST FOR GLOBAL DEVELOPMENT

Optimizing the Dynamic Conflict of Interest
in Transnational Migration

Binod Khadria

The so-called benefits that the developing countries of the
South supposedly derive from the migration of its people
may be classified as stereotypes that involve (1) the return
migration of workers with enhanced skills from the host
countries of the North to their home countries in the
South, (2) remittances, and (3) the transfer of technology
(Khadria 1990, 1999). Although there is a great deal of
discussion about the return migration of skilled people
to India, particularly in the wake of what is called business process outsourcing (BPO), the quantity and quality
of human capital returning to home countries are simply
not known. Similarly, while there are some estimates of
remittances that are available, along with the expectation
that they are substantial and will continue to increase,
most of these remittances are sent from countries of the
South itself—mainly, by unskilled migrants from the Gulf

countries of West Asia and the 'tiger economies' of East and Southeast Asia.[1] Moreover, the transfer of technology is controlled by a patent regime that is grossly tilted against the countries of the South. The TRIPS (Agreement on Trade-Related Aspects of Intellectual Property Rights), TRIMs (Agreement on Trade-Related Investment Measures), and GATS (General Agreement on Trade in Services) are the result of WTO (World Trade Organization) negotiations that have influenced the pricing of technology in a highly oligopolistic market. It can be argued that these three channels are the means through which the developed host countries of the North reap the maximum benefit from the immigration of highly skilled migrants from countries of the South, including India.

A case can be made, therefore, to think of an instrument whereby both a Southern country of origin and a counterpart Northern country of destination could be brought together for negotiations with a view to creating a 'win-win' situation, rather than 'harming' or being indifferent to each other. Such an instrument could be based on what could be termed an 'equitable adversary analysis' (see Applbaum 2000; Sen 1980, 1997). This involves stepping into each other's shoes and trying to defend the interests and position of the adversary rather than oneself. This would bring forth a better appreciation of the costs (or the likely 'injuries' or harm) to each of the two contending parties from the viewpoint of the other side rather than one's own, which normally occupies the minds of the negotiators in bilateral (and multilateral) negotiations. Adversary analysis would thus provide a more sympathetic evaluation of the problems associated with remittances that a source country receives and the problems of social harmony and unemployment possibly created in a destination country when its labor market is thronged with foreign skilled workers. However, what is required would be not only a level playing field but, going beyond that, an equitable commitment allowing the stronger party to have empathy for the weakness of the other side. In fact, the equitable adversary analysis as applied in migration need not be limited to bilateral negotiations; it could be custom-designed as a strategy of multilateral negotiations as well. All or most Southern countries could together represent the South as a whole, provided that this action is preceded by the successful consolidation of Southern interests through South-South cooperation.

As a Southern country of origin, India has drawn worldwide attention to the migration in the twenty-first century of so-called knowledge workers—mainly, information technology (IT) professionals—to developed countries, with 80 percent of the emigrants migrating to the United States. However, knowledge workers have been emigrating from India since the late 1960s (Khadria 2007b). Branded as 'brain drain', the migration of such highly educated Indians has been seen both as a financial 'investment loss' in education and as a social 'skill loss' of trained personnel (Khadria 2004). The exodus of those young unemployed graduates has also been viewed as the loss of potential reformists, who could bring about necessary political change in their own country (Khadria 2005). Conversely, the primary benefits of emigration have been identified as the return migration of those Indians who have been further educated and have acquired experience abroad, the monetary remittances sent home by the migrant workers, and the transfer of technology through programs such as the United Nations Development Programme's TOKTEN (Transfer of Knowledge Through Expatriate Nationals) program. However, the perceptions of subsequent Indian governments about these costs and benefits have undergone changes with shifts in the paradigm—from 'brain drain' in the 1960s and 1970s to 'brain bank' in the 1980s and

1990s and, subsequently, to 'brain gain' in the twenty-first century. This complete turnaround is reflected in the ongoing euphoria over increasing quotas for the immigration of skilled workers to developed countries, mainly, the United States, Canada, the United Kingdom, other countries in the European Union, Australia, and New Zealand.

Despite this enthusiasm, there are emerging contours of profit and loss (i.e., benefits and costs) in international migration that have remained uncharted so far (Khadria 2001, 2006a). Methodologically, these could be seen as arising from three key aspects of a dynamic conflict of interest among nations over international migration in the twenty-first century that are potentially very significant. I describe them in generic terms as 'age', 'wage', and 'vintage' (Khadria 2009).

The Dynamic Conflict of Interest between North and South

Age: The Primacy of Temporary Migration

In recent times, international migration policies of the developed Northern countries have shown a tendency to encourage even highly skilled Southern immigrants not to settle permanently in the destination country. Rather, these immigrants are influenced to 'circulate', that is, to shuttle between temporary modes of stay (in the host country) and return (to the home country). Migration has thus come to the point where older generations of human capital are moved and replaced by younger ones on a continuous basis, thus keeping the age profile of the immigrant worker population young. Among other benefits to host countries, this younger age profile neutralizes their own aging population structures.

Recent publications attest that in the twenty-first century the growth of permanent settler admissions in developed countries has slowed down, while the number of temporary worker entrants has grown more rapidly (OECD 2004). This is primarily a result of the new emphasis on return migration as part of the migration management policies instituted by the receiving Northern countries of Europe and the United States. In the case of legal migration, particularly involving educated and skilled migrants, the British work permit, the German 'green card', and the US H-1B non-immigrant visa—even the so-called GATS visa proposed by various WTO member countries—are all examples of policies invoked to encourage the temporary rather than permanent migration of highly skilled professionals.

Other developing countries of the South where emigrants originate, such as Pakistan, Bangladesh, and Sri Lanka in South Asia, have been overwhelmed by the bandwagon of a return migration policy, one which is said to benefit them in all respects. These countries have not shown enough internal sensitivity to comprehend the social costs of return migration policy on individual workers and their families, especially concerning unexpected violations of basic human rights and undesired outcomes in terms of human costs. For example, in most cases only the primary worker moves, and the immediate family tends to remain in the country of origin for much of the time. The family dilemma arises because of the possible constraints that the spouse's job and/or the children's schooling in the home country could put against giving it all up for only a temporary stay abroad. Under such circumstances, temporary migration entails a compulsory separation between the members of the family, making both the worker and the family 'nomadic' travelers due to the enhanced frequency at which they move to meet each other. Contract labor and temporary-visa migration also make the return of the worker to the home country a kind of 'forced' migration, although all the decisions within the concerned migrant's family tend to remain voluntary. Their acceptance and compliance have been eased by the shortening of long-distance communication and transport across borders.

Wage: The Silent Backwash of Remittances

According to the International Monetary Fund (IMF), remittances to developing countries were US $65 billion in 1999. In South Asian countries, remittances have grown very rapidly. For example, India, along with the Philippines, received 65 percent of inter-Asian remittances. The 2004 estimates of the World Bank (2005) recorded US $22 billion in remittances to India, close to 10 percent of the worldwide remittances sent home by 191 million migrants. This put India at the top of remittance-receiving countries, a position it continues to hold consistently, with remittances reaching US $52 billion in 2008 as per the latest data.[2] There is discussion surrounding the creation of policies to promote remittances, but not enough attention is being paid to the utilization of remittances in the home or sending countries and the ways they are ultimately captured by Northern banking institutions and multinational corporations located in the Southern countries.

In addition, the flow of funds to Northern countries as part of migration, such as those of international students, needs to be addressed. During his 2004 visit to the United Nations, Indian Prime Minister Dr. Manmohan Singh made an appeal to developed countries, such as the United Kingdom, to reduce their 'overseas student fees'—fees that are far higher than corresponding fees for their home students. There was a strong rationale behind the appeal in the fact that these developed countries were retaining the students on completion of their degrees for absorption in their own labor market. According to *Open Doors 2004: Report of International Educational Exchange*, published by the US Institute of International Education (IIE 2004), education funding for over two-thirds of the 572,509 international students in the United States in 2003–2004 was financed primarily by students' "personal and family" sources, while US sources supported only 25.7 percent of students. The latter share further fell to 24.4 percent for a higher number of 671,616 international students by 2008–2009 (IIE 2009).[3]

The US economy thus reaps a handsome US $13 billion annually from around 600,000 students who go to the United States to study. The IIE's (2005) data for 2004–2005 indicate that nearly 72 percent of all international students reported that their primary source of funding came from personal, family, or other sources outside of the United States. The proportion of students relying primarily on personal and family funding increased by 1.5 percentage points to 67 percent of all international students in the 2004–2005 year, and an even higher percentage—81 percent—was evident at the undergraduate level. Rising tuition costs and weak economies in some countries place a substantial economic burden on students and their families. On the other hand, US Department of Commerce data continue to rank US higher education among the five largest service sector exports. Similar estimates for the United Kingdom, other countries in the European Union, Canada, Australia, and New Zealand substantiate the proposition that developed receiving countries are already on the path to capitalize on the trade in educational services, even without GATS fully stepping in, and in this way to subsidize their own home students and their educational institutions (Khadria 2009: 119).[4]

As a result, there is now a new trend of a silent, back-wash flow of remittances out of the home countries of the migrants in the South to their host countries in the North. The home countries' short-sighted policies—or lack of any policy—are partly responsible for this development. For example, India, having amassed a huge amount of foreign exchange reserve, raised the permissible ceiling of US $25,000 per annum remittance abroad to US $50,000 at the end of 2006, and this has largely facilitated payment of the cost of educating Indian students abroad, now amounting to US $7 billion per year.[5]

Vintage: The Primacy of Student Migration

Highly skilled people from countries such as India have migrated not only through the employment gate but also through the academic gate—as "semi-finished human capital" (Majumdar 1994). Figures presented in the annual survey of the IIE (2004) reveal that during the 2003–2004 academic year, Indian students accounted for 13.9 percent of all foreign students in the United States, the largest percentage for the third year in a row, followed by China, Korea, Japan, Canada, and Taiwan. In the 2004–2005 academic year (IIE 2005), India remained the largest academic emigrant country of overseas students in the United States for the fourth consecutive year, with a total of 80,466 students. The figures indicate only a modest 1 percent increase over the prior year's enrollments—a rate of growth much slower than the double-digit increases of the previous three years. However, this modest increase was more than made up for by the increase of 23 percent from India, the largest among all countries, in the number of applications for fall 2006 overseas admissions, closely followed by China's 21 percent (*Hindustan Times*, 26 March 2006). India has continued this lead over the years.

In 2008–2009, Indian students, numbering 103,260 and registering a 9.2 percent increase over the previous year's enrollments, accounted for 15.4 percent of all foreign students in the United States, the largest percentage, followed by China, Korea, Canada, Japan, and Taiwan (IIE 2009). To serve the dual purpose of sustaining their expensive higher education structures and meeting short-term labor shortages, both the United States and the United Kingdom have adopted a policy of allowing international students to stay on and work, rather than return to their countries of origin upon completion of their degrees (*Hindustan Times*, 6 March 2005). However, much of this work is on temporary visas, allowing for the possibility that these graduates can be replaced by a more recently educated cohort. The growing competition among countries such as the United States, the United Kingdom, Canada, Australia, New Zealand, and Ireland, as well as non-English-speaking countries such as France, Germany, and the Netherlands, is attracting even Ivy League institutions to South Asia, particularly India, to recruit the best students (*The Economic Times*, 24 November 2004).

The effects of such key trends in countries of emigrant origin like India are evident in the shortage of teachers in leading institutions of professional higher education. The country's most prominent global brand, the publicly subsidized Indian Institutes of Technology (IITs), is starved for qualified teaching staff. Estimates suggest that some 380 critical vacancies at the seven IITs across the country had no takers (*The Economic Times*, 10 November 2004). With future teachers being wooed abroad, India could be left high and dry in its capacity to produce human capital, the backbone of the country's advantage in IT, biotechnology, and so on. Meanwhile, the Northern countries selectively accumulate the latest vintage of knowledge and technology embodied in the most recent generations of students.[6] In addition, destination countries also gain political mileage in the form of foreign students who become their long-term ambassadors in the international political arena.

Between Return Migration and Naturalization: The Emerging Institution of Dual Citizenship

Paradoxically, along with the direct promotion of temporary migration policies aimed at the return of migrants to their home countries, the twenty-first century has also witnessed the issue of dual citizenship appearing on the agenda of nations (see table 1)—both immigrant-receiving and immigrant-sending countries—along with the promotion of naturalization and the reinstatement of lost citizenship (see Faist and Kivisto 2008). Examples of impacts, either direct or indirect, of this trend to recognize multiple identities in policy circles of the receiving Northern countries include the fact that (1) in North America, the US Census 2000 counted persons with 'more than one race'; (2) in Europe, the British Census 2001 counted ethnic groups and persons 'born abroad'; and (3) in the Pacific, in 2002, the Australian government liberalized its stance toward dual nationality. Examples of similar changes being made in sending countries in the South include the following: (1) in Southeast Asia, the lifting of a ban on dual citizenship in the Philippines in 2003; (2) in South Asia, the granting of Overseas Citizenship of India (OCI) in 2005; and (3) in Eurasia, the ongoing debate in Armenia over dual citizenship (AIPRG 2006).

Interestingly, by way of encouraging to-and–fro mobility, or what is presently known as 'circulatory migration', between nation-states in which a migrant settler holds citizenships, dual citizenship leads to a kind of reversal from permanent to temporary migration, although with a difference. This difference would arise primarily from the return migration to the country of origin (i.e., the flow that is intrinsic in temporary migration) becoming more voluntary and less permanent in nature.[7] The newly intensified circulatory migration would thus involve what may be appropriately called 'temporary return' to the country of origin, as opposed to a permanent return, once and for all. In properly understanding the fallout of this paradoxical reversal of focus from return migration per se to temporary return, one needs to refer back to the generic costs and benefits (to the host and home countries) elaborated earlier—that is, the determinants that would drive their policies toward or away from dual citizenship, particularly in the context of the political economy of transnationalization and development.

The growing phenomenon of business process outsourcing (BPO) to these low-income (and therefore low labor-cost) economies of South Asia is also being projected as a joint product of return migration policies at the upper end of the skill spectrum, popularly called the brain gain.[8] There is an important distinction between the two, however, that needs to be taken note of. An incidence of return under a return migration policy has social costs that a return under market forces may not have because of the degree of constraint involved—ranging between compulsion and autonomy—in the decision making about emigration and/or return to the country of origin, with compulsion being high in the former and minimal in the latter.

The major contrast is that under temporary migration, the tendency of change is toward eventual return of the migrant, whereas under permanent migration, it is toward naturalization. It is the latter that, when accompanied by dual citizenship, would encourage return migration through circulation and not compulsion. A return migration policy vis-à-vis dual citizenship has very different social costs to individual workers and their families in comparison to the many deprivations experienced by those offered only the possibility of temporary migration. In temporary migration arrangements, such as the Live-in Caregiver Program (LCP) in Canada, women migrant workers from the Philippines have to remain separated from their families for years and sometimes decades. Dual citizenship would, in this respect, be more likely to eliminate the degree of compulsion that is contained in the 'induced return' or 'forced return' of temporary work visas and to replace it with the 'voluntary temporary return', which in turn would lead to circulatory migration.

The costs and benefits of dual citizenship are perceived by states in terms of an array of equity and efficiency elements that include loyalty; an exit option for some members (i.e., when dual nationals have an option that most others within the nation's citizenry would not enjoy); unfairness of double voting; instructed voting; costs arising from the heterogeneity of diplomatic protection, military service, and conscription; and conflict of law regarding civil status, inheritance, taxation, and pension benefits. The presumed benefits would include revived affiliations and connections with home countries and the promotion of voluntary naturalization and integration in the host countries. These could all be analyzed more generically in the context of a policy emphasis toward a full circle. Such an approach would alter the status of most migrants from that of a temporary immigrant to that of a permanent resident, a naturalized citizen, a dual/multiple citizen, and, lastly, a circular migrant (in effect, a temporary returnee) (see fig. 1).

An extremely fast-track example of such a policy transition among recipient countries is currently visible in the growing primacy of student immigration in the developed

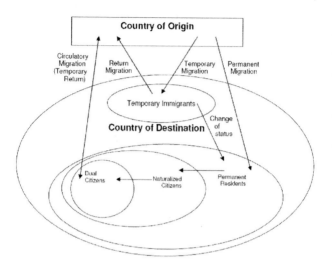

FIGURE 1 The Cycle of Migration for Development—Dual Citizenship–Induced Circulatory Migration and Temporary Return

receiving countries. Students are normally admitted on temporary visas in most countries, but the growing competition among developed countries for enrolling foreign students has brought admissions officials of Northern higher education institutions to Asian countries, in particular, to low-income South Asia (*The Economic Times*, 24 November 2004; see also Khadria 2002, 2006c). To serve the dual purpose—that is, to sustain their expensive higher education systems and to meet short-term labor shortages—both the United States and the United Kingdom have recently adopted a policy of allowing foreign students to stay on and work, rather than forcing them to return to their countries of origin on completion of their degrees. In New Zealand, and more recently in Singapore, policies have been announced to encourage foreign students to take up jobs at the end of their studies, to be followed by permanent status and eventual citizenship. The immanent brain drain would perhaps have an opportunity to be mitigated if naturalization gave way to dual citizenship, which would facilitate circulatory migration so that the diaspora could engage in the development of both host and home countries, rather than only that of the former.[9]

Territorial Limits of Diasporic Resources: The Macro Canvas of Development Engagement through South-South Cooperation

The informal or formal acceptance of dual nationality can increase the availability of rights for migrants in a fast-changing global society. Innovations can take it further in, heuristically speaking, fostering South-South cooperation among low-income countries. Hypothetically speaking, dual citizenship could even pave the way for the dual citizens of each of these countries, living in a third country of the North, to come together to develop policies of return whereby the returning nationals would not always be encouraged to return to their own low-income homeland every time they wished to engage their skill, labor, and time in a development program, but rather could do so in a poor third country. This could contribute to intra-South development-related transnationalism.[10] By its inherent characteristics, the granting of dual citizenship to an individual at the micro level by one state involves transnational recognition of the sovereignty of the other state upon its members at the micro level and, therefore, indirectly of the maxim of mutual co-existence at the macro level. As an extrapolation of this latent relationship between countries, it becomes possible to think of dual citizenship as a possible route to South-South cooperation for transnational development.

One perhaps cannot generalize, but surely dual citizenship could play a role in initiating or strengthening South-South cooperation for development-related projects by bringing different nationalities of origin together, creating a multi-polar link of diasporic relations between citizens of different countries residing in a single host country (Faist and Kivisto 2008). For example, an Indian-American dual citizen in the United States could become the medium of arbitration and cooperation between the two governments of India and China when his or her colleague is a Chinese-American citizen through whom he or she could lobby the Chinese government. Such a bilateral situation could also be duplicated multilaterally when 'club members' of naturalized American citizens hold two citizenships—one from the United States and the other from one of the various Asian countries of their origin. When dual citizenship is not allowed by the countries of origin, the members would have neither the legitimacy nor a strong enough emotional bond to become involved in such endeavors. For voluntary NGO activities, the scope of such cooperation would be even greater. In fact, the to-and-fro circular migration between host and home countries, as facilitated by dual citizenship, could then be further extended to make possible the triangular or quadrilateral or even multilateral circular migration of a dual national, involving a country of which he or she is not a citizen but whose co-member in the club is (see fig. 2). This would enable the engagement of the diaspora resources in what I would call 'third country development' in many poor nations of the South.

To operationalize such cooperation between members of the Southern countries, it should be possible to create regional or sub-continental umbrella networks of the

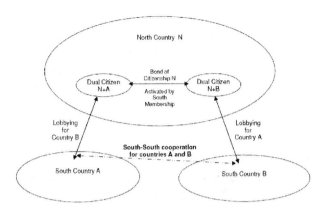

FIGURE 2 South-South Cooperation through Dual Citizenship

diasporas across countries. Other than overseas Chinese investing in homeland China, as an example of such possible intra-South transnationalization, the Korean diaspora has invested in host land China. The rapid economic growth of South Korea has made it a significant source of foreign investment in China. One Chinese region that has received significant attention from South Korean investors is the Yanbian Prefecture. Bordering North Korea, it has a total population that has increased from 0.83 million in 1950 to 2.14 million by 1993. While Koreans are still the largest ethnic group in Yanbian, as a proportion of the total population, they have steadily declined from 63 percent in 1949 to 40 percent in 1993. Nevertheless, available information indicates that the South Korean diaspora is still the principal one that bestows its resources on the Chinese prefecture and its towns (Wu 1998: 94–97).

Still, there is a flip side to the prospects of such South-South cooperation that one must keep in mind. Ideally, any analysis of dual citizenship that focuses on low-income

Southern countries should incorporate the legal provisions as well as the incidence of dual citizenship for its nationals abroad. However, intra-South dual citizenship would perhaps be discouraged for in-migrants in receiving countries, although it would be welcome for emigrants from overpopulated or poor sending countries as a South-South cooperation strategy. This leaves the domain of dual citizenship limited to emigrants as opposed to immigrants in the Southern countries.

Having explored these possibilities, the next question for South-South cooperation would be to determine the kind of development to engage in: top-down, through the involvement of a few business and industry leaders, or bottom-up, through education and improving the health of the masses. The top-down approach would certainly have costs, including the possible marginalization and exclusion of the lowest-income countries within the South. The bottom-up approach would be inclusive of them but would require a longer gestation period. In the first option, better-off intra-South diasporas would have the capabilities to use dual citizenship mainly to their advantage, whereas the worse-off would be left out; in the latter option, they would use their capabilities to uplift the poorer countries. There is thus scope for complementarities. What is perhaps required, *through* and *for* South-South cooperation, is a long-term policy that is aimed at establishing a link with a pan-South diaspora for sustainable socio-economic development, where inter-country exchange and cooperation are inbuilt. This could take place through a fusion between economic groups such as the Association of Southeast Asian Nations (ASEAN), the South Asian Association for Regional Cooperation (SAARC), and other such alliances.[11]

To arrive at the proverbial 'win-win-win' situation in intra-regional relations through South-South cooperation for all three stakeholders (the countries of origin in the South, the migrants as a pan-South diaspora, and the host destination countries of the high-income North), two specific conditions must be met: (1) a 'necessary condition' of the dominant or significant global geo-economic presence of Southern workers, and (2) a 'sufficient condition' whereby the home countries in the South derive sustainable benefits from the global presence of the Southern migrants. In terms of the large demand abroad for skilled and unskilled workers from the South and the fact that Southern migrants have established excellent records of accomplishment in the countries of their settlement, it can be said with some degree of confidence that the first, necessary condition has been more or less fulfilled.[12] To satisfy the second, sufficient condition, though, the diaspora resources such as the flows of remittances, cross-country transfers of technology, and return and circular migration must not all be directed toward trade and business. Rather, they should be substantially directed toward the removal of two kinds of poverty in the region—the 'poverty of education' and the 'poverty of health'.

In these two areas, the improvement of which would contribute to economic and social development, migration has so far failed society in Southern countries of origin. Large masses of the illiterate and uneducated population, incapacitated further by their poor health status, are the root causes of the South having some of the lowest levels of average productivity of labor and therefore the lowest average wages in the world. This is a paradox, considering that members of their diasporas, such as Indians or Chinese or Filipinos, individually and on the average, make up the largest contributing single ethnic communities in their countries of destination.[13] South-South diaspora networks and associations abroad could, therefore, through state intervention, play the catalyst's role in raising the average productivity of the mass of Southern workers in their respective home countries by looking on health and education as Millennium Development Goals (MDGs)— that is, priority areas of diaspora engagement—rather than focusing on immediate but unstable profit-making ventures in industry and business.

Are there lessons to be learned from within Asia here? Is it not wise to try to imitate China's bottom-up path that it followed long ago through mass education and health care initiatives and not getting carried away by its present top-down path of leveraging the 'diaspora capital' for development? Perhaps the answer would lie somewhere in between. Given the speed of globalization, low-income countries of the South, such as India, do not have an either-or choice in this matter with regard to long-term bottom-up or short-term top-down deployments of diaspora resources. They will have to choose a middle path by combining short- and long-run strategies of development, focusing on business and industry for the short-term targets of immediate employment generation and on education and health as long-term objectives for generating employable human capital, with the latter geared toward raising and sustaining the average productivity of labor at home. Such a mix would ameliorate many migration woes as it would allow the sending countries of the South to acquire immunity to emigration. It could also help them deal with immigration as well, since a highly productive labor force could more adequately feed the poor immigrants pouring in from even lower-income neighboring countries. The new century has marked a paradigm shift through globalization to which the policy discourse of the South must adjust and from which it can benefit.

This sets a 'double challenge' of public policy for the sending countries of the South. First, they must convince their own diaspora communities abroad to rethink the development process in their homeland as a bottom-up creation and enhancement of sustainable productivities of labor through the development of education and health rather than a top-down achievement through participation in business and industry. One process is comprehensive, the other dispersed; one is long-term, the other immediate. This would involve not only a matter of willingness. In many instances, it would entail long periods of struggle to create those decision-making and priority-setting capabilities among discerning leaders of the migrant community to appreciate the logic that a large population with purchasing power in pocket would provide the sustainable market in which they would be able to sell their products more effectively and profitably than in a large population with no purchasing power. Secondly, they must be able to convince the countries of destination in the North (and the other countries of origin within the South as well) as to where the distinction lies between the most 'painful' and the most 'gainful' socio-economic impacts of the migration of citizens, whether skilled or unskilled. For the high-income receiving countries of the North, the winning situation would arise because these destination countries would then be able to continue to attract knowledge workers—both young professionals and youthful students—from Southern countries. This ameliorates their own problems of an aging population with pension liabilities and sustains their lead in the accumulation of the latest vintages of knowledge as embodied in the latest generations of graduates and students (Khadria 2006c).

Such adversary analysis of costs as well as benefits in multilateral forums would help countries of the South press for international norms in the Mode 4 negotiations of the GATS on the issue of the movement of 'natural persons' as service providers under trade, which is simply another description for propagating the temporary entry route for non-nationals, as opposed to circular mobility through permanent migration and dual citizenship. That the temporary route—operationalized by the 'open and shut' migration policies of the recipient countries of the North—has been full of vulnerabilities for migrants at the micro level (those beginning with the varying consular practices) and leads to instabilities of the 'cobweb disequilibrium' variety in migrants' education and labor markets at the macro level must be conveyed emphatically. One way of taking the first concrete steps toward upholding a demand for guaranteed removal of these two key elements from practice would perhaps be that the Southern countries must not only contemplate but actually demonstrate South-South cooperation, or rather solidarity, on dual citizenship among themselves. Possibilities emerging from new configurations, such as the BRIC (Brazil, Russia, India, China) political bloc, could be the grounds for such hope about South-South cooperation.[14]

Lessons to be Learned: Methodological Locus of Three Issues

In trying to understand who reaps the benefits from the policy transition that is currently underway, I would thus urge that we visualize a locus of three central issues that encompass the paradigm shift in migration today: labor transfer, financial transfer, and knowledge transfer.

First, migration concerns with regard to the aging population structures in the developed countries primarily underlie the labor market mismatches, prompting policies that prefer youth immigration to fill the quantitative physical gaps of numbers. The soaring migration of medicos, nurses, and caregivers to look after the ailing and the aged, health tourism, etc., are part of this group of labor transfer issues.

Second, there are wage concerns related to temporary migration replacing permanent migration, the former leading to a higher turnover of migrant workers and thus slower growth of the overall wages bills, perks, and pension commitments to foreign workers in countries of destination. The dynamics of remittances and the tax liabilities of migrant workers also form part of this group of financial transfer issues.

The third issue concerns the competitive agendas and strategies of nations to accumulate quality human capital. The goal is to generate the latest vintages of knowledge through cost-effective talent flows embodied in the mobility of professionals and graduate students in cutting-edge areas such as information technology, bio-technology, and a variety of other fields. National security concerns of the post-9/11 immigration regimes and issues such as dual citizenship also belong to this genre of knowledge transfer issues, including globalization or segmentation of the curriculum between citizens and foreigners.

To draw a comparison between the present time and the decades between 1965 and 1995, one noticeable difference is that the center of focus has shifted from source-country determinants of migration in the South to destination-country determinants in the North. Today, migration flows are formidably demand-determined and worker-seeking, as opposed to being supply-determined and work-seeking as they were, for example, 30 years ago. It is now a challenging area where the conflict of interest between the countries of the North and the South is no longer static but dynamic—the interests of the former and the latter extending over significantly different time horizons. Why is migration now an area that the countries consider 'non-negotiable sovereign territory' when it comes to multilateral discussions in which policy makers of the North and the South can actually try to influence each other's decisions, whether by lobbying or moral suasion? Only an equitable adversary analysis of the dynamic conflict of interest would succeed in bringing these matters to the table for an optimal, balanced, and equitable 'inter-transnationalization' between the countries of the North and the South. Otherwise, the Northern countries would perhaps generate an 'intra-transnationalization' among themselves from which the Southern countries would be excluded.

Acknowledgments

This essay is based on the author's paper presented at the conference, "Transnationalization and Development(s): Towards a North-South Perspective," at the Center for Interdisciplinary Research, Bielefeld University, 31 May–1 June 2007. The author is grateful to Thomas Faist, Nina Glick Schiller, and an anonymous referee for comments on an earlier draft.

Notes

1. For remittance figures for various years, see publications of the Reserve Bank of India at http://www.rbi.org.in/SCRIPTS/Publications.aspx.
2. See the Migration and Remittances Factbook compiled by Dilip Ratha and Zhimei Xu, Migration and Remittances Team, World Bank. See http://siteresources.worldbank.org/INTPROSPECTS/Resources/334934-1199807908806/Top10.pdf (accessed 26 June 2009).
3. US sources included "US College or University" (22.7%), "US Government" (0.6%), and "US Private Sponsor" (1.1%). Personal, family, or other sources were "Personal and Family Funds" (64.9%), "Home Government/University" (3.7%), "Foreign Private Sponsor" (0.9%), "International Organization" (0.2%), "Current Employment" (5.0%), and "Others" (0.9%).

4. This raises the average cost of education, thereby adversely affecting the competitiveness of foreign students and their countries of origin in the global labor markets. There is a corollary in this to the United States subsidizing its cotton growers, thereby hurting and marginalizing those in Africa and Brazil (Stiglitz 2006). For a survey of student enrollments in science streams in India, see Shukla (2005).

5. See "FDI in Education Top Priority: Kapil Sibal," *The Times of India,* 25 June 2009, http://timesofindia.indiatimes.com/India/FDI-in-education-top-priority-Kapil-Sibal/articleshow/4700695.cms (accessed 4 July 2009).

6. See, for example, the provision of a Technology Alert List (TAL) in the US immigration policy with regard to the issuance of visas to students and exchange visitors, http://www. usafis. org/us-immigration/glossary-definitions.asp.

7. While for most developing countries the return of talent is unrealistic, so-called brain circulation networks can be developed to create conditions for expatriates to engage with their home countries, in particular in the areas of knowledge transfer, business creation, and the promotion of technology-intensive foreign direct investment (FDI). There are three main types of 'brain circulation': diaspora networks of scientists and research and development personnel, business networks of innovative start-ups, and networks of professionals working for multinationals. To be efficacious for the home countries, each of these networks has to be designed in accordance with its own characteristics. Scientific networks, for instance, are quite easy to start but difficult to sustain, while the opposite is true for influential professionals in multinationals (see Kuznetsov 2006).

8. See, for example, BBC News, "Viewpoints: Should Borders be Open?" 13 April 2004, http://news.bbc.co.uk/1/hi/in_depth/3512992.stm (accessed on 13 April 2009); BBC News, "Born Abroad: An Immigration Map of Britain," 9 September 2005, http://news.bbc.co.uk/2/shared/spl/hi/uk/05/born_abroad/countries/html/india.stm (accessed on 24 August 2009); BBC News, "India Attracts Western Tech Talent," by Zubair Ahmad, 5 September 2006, http://news.bbc.co.uk/2/hi/south_asia/5272672.stm. See also Khadria (2006b, 2006d).

9. There are no hard data yet, but the Indian government's initiative of introducing a partial dual citizenship through Overseas Citizenship of India (OCI) has actually encouraged higher

circulatory migration of the Indian diaspora members to Indian cities for durations long enough to participate in development projects. Indian Prime Minister Manmohan Singh has been quoted as saying, "I am therefore happy to announce that henceforth OCI (Overseas Citizenship of India) card holders who are qualified professionals—doctors, dentists, pharmacists, engineers, architects and chartered accountants—will have the benefit of practicing their professions in India." See http://forums.sulekha.com/forums/coffeehouse/Overseas-Indian-professionals-can-work-in-India-PM-910637.htm (accessed 7 July 2009).

10. For example, the Indian Spinal Injuries Centre (ISIC), which also houses returning Indian doctors, is setting up the Kenya Spinal Injuries Centre (KSIC) in Nairobi. The ISIC chairperson, Major H. P. S. Ahluwalia, says, "Africa lacks facilities for spinal injury management. By helping KSIC set up a facility ... ISIC hopes to reach out to not only spinal injury patients in Kenya but also to people from other neighbouring countries who routinely come there for treatment. If this initiative is success-ful, it will set the trend for many such centres to come up in different parts of Africa and around the world." See "Medical Centre in Kenya to Be Set up with Indian Assistance," *The Hindu*, 7 July 2009, http://www.thehindu.com/2009/07/07/stories/2009070759020400.htm.

11. See the July 2007 special issue of *Asian Population Studies* (Khadria 2007a).

12. Whichever approach is chosen, the engagement of diaspora resources would depend on the capability of the members of the diaspora group to actually participate in such endeavors. One example could be the length of stay in the host country (see Chiswick 1978). In other words, capabilities for development engagement of the diaspora would be the indices of access to the enabling determinants, with or without dual citizenship. Such 'capabilities' à la Amartya Sen (1999) could, in this case, be measured by indices of how much of the geo-economic space the Southern diasporas occupy in the receiving country. For example, in the United States, the US census data may be used as proxies of such capabilities.

13. It is indeed paradoxical that the average per hour contribu-tion of each employed worker within India to the production of India's gross domestic product (GDP) has been among the

lowest in the world—a mere 37 cents, one-hundredth of that of the US average of $37. This is naturally ironic because the same average Indian employed abroad contributes a very high average share to the GDP of the country where he or she settles and works (Khadria 2002).

14. For a discussion on the formation of the BRIC bloc, see http://www.timesonline.co.uk/tol/news/world/us_and_americas/article6514737.ece.

References

AIPRG (Armenian International Policy Research Group). 2006. "Dual Citizenship: Alternative Arrangements, Economic Implications, and Social Dimensions." Press release on a conference held on 17–18 June, at Yerevan, Armenia. http://www.aiprg.net (accessed 22 June 2009).

Applbaum, Anthony I. 2000. *Ethics for Adversaries: The Morality of Roles in Public and Professional Life.* Princeton, NJ: Princeton University Press.

Chiswick, Barry R. 1978. "The Effects of Americanization on the Earnings of Foreign-Born Men." *Journal of Political Economy* 86, no. 5: 897–921.

Faist, Thomas, and Peter Kivisto, eds. 2008. *Dual Citizenship in Global Perspective: From Unitary to Multiple Citizenship.* Houndmills: Palgrave Macmillan.

IIE (Institute of International Education). 2004. *Open Doors 2004: Report of International Educational Exchange.* Washington, DC: Institute of International Education.

_____. 2005. *Open Doors 2005: Report of International Educational Exchange.* Washington, DC: Institute of International Education.

_____. 2009. *Open Doors 2009: Report of International Educational Exchange.* Washington, DC: Institute of International Education.

Khadria, Binod. 1990. "Patents, Brain Drain and Higher Education: International Barriers to the Diffusion of Knowledge, Information and Technology." *Social Scientist* 18, no. 5: 3–18.

_____. 1999. *The Migration of Knowledge Workers: Second-Generation Effects of India's Brain Drain.* New Delhi: Sage Publications.

_____. 2001. "Shifting Paradigm of Globalization: The Twenty-First Century Transition towards Generics in Skilled Migration from India." *International Migration* 39, no. 5: 45–71.

_____. 2002. "Skilled Labour Migration from Developing Countries: Study on India." International Migration Papers, No. 49, Geneva: International Labour Office (ILO).

_____. 2004. "Human Resources in Science and Technology in India and the International Mobility of Highly Skilled Indians." STI Working Paper 2004/7, OECD, Paris, May.

_____. 2005. "Migration in South and South-West Asia," Regional Study No. RS 6, Policy Analysis and Research Programme of the Global Commission on International Migration, Geneva, September.

_____. 2006a. "Uncharted Contours of a Changing Paradigm: Skilled Migration and Brain Drain in India." *Harvard International Review* 28, no. 1. Web-exclusive Symposium on featured topic: immigration. http://www.hir.harvard.edu (accessed 13 October 2009)

_____. 2006b. "'Post-War Migration,' 'Migration of Professionals,' and 'Business and Entrepreneurs.'" Pp. 66–75, 80–81 in *The Encyclopedia of the Indian Diaspora*, ed. Brij Lal. Singapore: Editions Didier Millet.

_____. 2006c. "Embodied and Disembodied Transfers of Knowledge: Geo-politics of Economic Development." Pp. 191–203 in *Knowledge for Development*, ed. Michel Carton and Jean-Baptiste Meyer, Paris: l'Harmattan.

_____. 2006d. "Migration between India and the UK." *Public Policy Research* 13, no. 3: 172–184.

_____. 2007a. "Guest Editor's Introduction." *Asian Population Studies* 3, no. 2: 99–101.

_____. 2007b. "Tracing the Genesis of Brain Drain in India through Its State Policy and Civil Society." Pp. 265–282 in *Citizenship and Those Who Leave: The Politics of Emigration and Expatriation*, ed. Nancy L. Green and François Weil. Urbana, IL: University of Illinois Press.

_____, ed. 2009. *India Migration Report 2009: Past, Present and the Future Outlook*. New Delhi: International Migration and Diaspora Studies Project, JNU.

Kuznetsov, Yuri, ed. 2006. *Diaspora Networks and the International Migration of Skills: How Countries Can Draw on Their Talent Abroad*. Washington, DC: World Bank.

Majumdar, Tapas. 1994. "Old World is the New World." *The Telegraph*, Calcutta, 8 August.

OECD (Organisation for Economic Co-operation and Development). 2004. *Trends in International Migration: Annual Report 2003 Edition*. Paris: Organisation for Economic Co-operation and Development.

Sen, Amartya. 1980. "Labour and Technology." Pp. 121–158 in *Policies for Industrial Progress in Developing Countries*, ed. John Cody, Helen Hughes, and David Wall. Oxford: Oxford University Press.

_____. 1997. "Policy-Making and Social Choice Pessimism." Pp. 3–22 in *Issues in Economic Theory and Public Policy: Essays in Honour of Professor Tapas Majumdar*, ed. Amitava Bose, Mihir Rakshit, and Anup Sinha. New Delhi: Oxford University Press.

_____. 1999. *Development as Freedom*. Oxford: Oxford University Press.

Shukla, Rajesh. 2005. *India Science Report*. New Delhi: National Council of Applied Economic Research.

Stiglitz, Joseph, 2006. *Making Globalization Work*. London: Allen Lane.

World Bank. 2005. *World Economic Outlook*. Washington, DC: World Bank.

Wu, Chung-Tong. 1998. "Diaspora Investments and Their Regional Impacts in China." Pp. 77–105 in *Regional Change in Industrializing Asia: Regional and Local Responses to Changing Competitiveness*, ed. Leo van Grunsven. Aldershot: Ashgate.

CONTRIBUTORS

Raúl Delgado Wise is Director of the Development Studies Doctoral Program at the Autonomous University of Zacatecas (Mexico) and President of the International Migration and Development Network. He is the author/editor of 14 books and more than 100 essays, including book chapters and refereed articles. In 1993, he was the recipient of the Maestro Jesús Silva Herzog award for economics research. He has been a guest lecturer in North, Central, and South America and the Caribbean, Europe, Canada, Africa, and Asia. He is a member of the Mexican Academy of Sciences, of the National System of Researchers, and of several scholarly associations in Canada, the United States, Latin America, and Europe. He is co-editor of the journal *Migración y Desarrollo*, a member of the editorial committee of several academic journals in the US, Chile, Argentina, and Mexico, and editor of the book series "Latin America and the New World Order" for Miguel Angel Porrúa.

Thomas Faist is Professor of Transnational and Development Studies in the Department of Sociology, Bielefeld University. His research interests focus on international migration, immigrant integration, citizenship, social policy, and development studies. His current research deals with environmental degradation and migration and the transnational social question. He serves on the editorial board of *The Sociological Quarterly*, *Ethnic and Racial Studies*, *Migration Letters*, and *South*

Asian Diaspora. He recently published *Citizenship: Discourse, Theory, and Transnational Prospects* (with co-author Peter Kivisto, 2007) and *Dual Citizenship in Global Perspective: From Unitary to Multiple Citizenship* (with co-editor Peter Kivisto, 2008). He also edited *Dual Citizenship in Europe: From Nationhood to Societal Integration* (2007) and co-edited *The Europeanization of National Policies and Politics of Immigration* (with Andreas Ette, 2007).

Nina Glick Schiller is Director of the Cosmopolitan Cultures Institute and Professor of Social Anthropology at the University of Manchester. Her fields of interest include transnational migration, diasporic connection, long-distance nationalism, and comparative perspectives on city rescaling and migration. The founding editor of the journal *Identities: Global Studies in Culture and Power*, Glick Schiller has published *Towards a Transnational Perspective on Migration* (1992) and *Nations Unbound* (1994) (both with Linda Basch and Cristina Szanton Blanc), and *Georges Woke Up Laughing* (2001) (with Georges Fouron). Her research has been conducted in Haiti, the United States, and Germany, and she has worked with migrants from all over the globe.

Riina Isotalo has researched different aspects of Palestinian transnationality in the context of conflict as well as post-conflict social and political issues, such as citizenship practices and gender. She wrote her PhD dissertation in social anthropology on Palestinian return, transnationalism, and gender in 2005, and has published articles and book chapters on Palestinian return migration, transnational lifestyles and family dynamics, identity politics with regard to the issues of refugees, and post-conflict return and the relations among gender, legal pluralism, and international post-conflict assistance. She has taught courses and seminars on gender, development, and reflexive methodologies. She is presently a researcher on Gender Studies in Law at the University of Helsinki.

Binod Khadria is Professor of Economics and Director of the International Migration and Diaspora Studies Project at the Zakir Husain Centre for Educational Studies, School of Social Sciences, Jawaharlal Nehru University, New Delhi. He is the author of *The Migration of Knowledge Workers: Second-Generation Effects of India's Brain Drain* (1999), and his research on migration has been published by various organizations, including the ILO, OECD, Institut de Recherche pour le Développement, Institute of Developing Economies–Japan External Trade Organization, and Global Commission on International Migration, to name a few. Apart from international migration, his research and teaching interests are in the economics of education, trade in services, and development. Widely traveled, he has been a visiting scholar at a number of universities around the world. He was a nominated member of the International Advisory Committee for the 3rd Global Forum on Migration and Development held at Athens in November 2009, and is on the Editorial Board of *Asia-Pacific Migration Journal*. Recently, he has edited and launched the *India Migration Report 2009*, the inaugural issue of the annual publication.

Humberto Márquez Covarrubias is Professor of the Development Studies Doctoral Program at the Autonomous University of Zacatecas and a member of the National Research System, the International Network on Migration and Development, and the Mexican Association of Rural Studies. He has published numerous essays, book chapters, and journal articles on topics related to development and migration and is currently co-editor of the journal *Migración y Desarrollo*.